If These WALLS Could TALK:
PHILADELPHIA FLYERS

If These **WALLS** Could **TALK:**

PHILADELPHIA FLYERS

Stories from the
Philadelphia Flyers Ice,
Locker Room, and Press Box

Lou Nolan and Sam Carchidi

TRIUMPH
BOOKS

Library of Congress Cataloging-in-Publication Data available upon request

This book is available in quantity at special discounts for your group or organization. For further information, contact:

Triumph Books LLC
814 North Franklin Street
Chicago, Illinois 60610
www.triumphbooks.com

Printed in U.S.A.

ISBN: 978-1-62937-406-2

Design by Amy Carter

Page Production by Nord Compo

Photos courtesy of Lou Nolan unless otherwise indicated

To my wife, Ellen, and sons, Matt and Jeff,
for all their loving support and for being real Flyers fans.

And to the late Ed Snider, Lou Scheinfeld, and my great friend,
Joe Kadlec, who allowed me to have so much fun
with the Flyers and their fans.

—Lou Nolan

To my wife and best friend, JoAnn, for putting up with my crazy hours
all these years. Without the support of her and my children,
Sara and Sammy, my work would seem fruitless. Thanks, guys.
You're the best! You, too, Brian and Maryann.

—Sam Carchidi

CONTENTS

FOREWORD

When you've been around hockey most of your life, as I have, you get to meet some wonderful people.

Like the great Lou Nolan.

I count my blessings that I can call Lou one of my close friends. We go back to 1967–68, the Flyers' inaugural season.

In Philadelphia, Lou isn't just the friendly voice we have come to know and respect during his many years as the Flyers public address announcer. He is a man of great integrity and values, a man who has a beautiful association with Flyers fans.

Lou has been with the Flyers longer than anyone—the 2016–17 season was his 50th year with the club—and that speaks volumes about his professionalism. You don't last that long unless you're a true pro.

I always ask people, "What is it you love to do in life?" And if I were to ask Lou that question, he would say, without any hesitation, just what he is doing right now. And that's why he has lasted so long in this profession. It never gets old. It's always exciting. You can hear it in his voice and in the way he presents himself.

I am grateful to have been around Lou for so long. We've done a number of different appearances together over the years, and Lou has always been kind, has always been smiling, has always been positive, and has always been great to be around.

I know he has experienced so much during his half century with the Flyers, and I'm so happy he decided to share those experiences with the public.

There's too much negativity in the world today, but Lou is an example of everything that is positive and wonderful about life.

It's a beautiful thing.

—Bernie Parent

Goaltender Bernie Parent led the Philadelphia Flyers to Stanley Cups in 1974 and 1975, and he had shutouts in both of the clinching wins. In 1984, Parent became the first Flyer inducted into the Hockey Hall of Fame, and in 2017, as part of the NHL's 100th anniversary, he was selected as one of the top 100 players in the league's history.

Photo courtesy of the Philadelphia Flyers.

ACKNOWLEDGMENTS

T hanks go out to Augie Conte and his crew of NHL off-ice officials, who always get me the timely information I share with the fans.

Also, thanks to Flyers public relations director Zack Hill for his help, and to Anthony Gioia, Artie Halstead, and the techs in ArenaVision who keep me on the air.

To countless Flyers players, past and present, who gave us thrills on the ice for 50 years plus.

To Lou Scheinfeld, who set up an audition during third-level construction of the Spectrum and put me at center ice on the mic.

And, finally, to Sam Carchidi, with whom the idea for this book was born, and who took my words and brought them to life.

—L.N.

A special thanks to my late Uncle George, who took me to my first Flyers game in 1967—the year the team was born—and helped me get hooked on the sport.

And a heartfelt thank you to Lou Nolan, an Original Flyer who never ran out of wonderful stories and is the man who made this book a reality. Thanks for making this such a joyful project, Lou!

—S.C.

CHAPTER 1

THE START OF AN "INCREDIBLE JOURNEY"

F or a lot of years, selling securities to banks has been my *real* job. But my most rewarding job has been the one that, for a half century, has taken me inside a noisy, percolating South Philadelphia hockey arena during the fall, winter, and spring months.

I have been fortunate enough to have been with the Flyers since their inception in 1967—first as a public relations assistant to Joe Kadlec, and then, since 1972, as their public address announcer.

It's a career that has been fulfilling, exhilarating, and unpredictable. Witness my first game as public address announcer. There I was, minding my own business and sitting between two players who went to the Spectrum penalty box during a preseason game. They were yapping at each other as they sat down when, suddenly, the visiting player picked up a bucket of ice and heaved it at our guy, Bob Kelly, who was one of our feisty wingers.

The ice never reached the player they called Hound. Instead, it bounced off the side of my head and drenched my sport coat as the fans sitting behind us let out a collective roar.

In a way, it was my baptism into the NHL. Instead of holy water, I got christened with ice water. Hey, just part of the job. Part of what has been an incredible journey.

The Flyers finished with their first winning record in franchise history during my first year as the PA announcer, and that started an amazing stretch during which Philadelphia fell in love with the Orange and Black.

I have witnessed some great moments along the way: eight trips to the Stanley Cup Finals, consecutive championships in 1974 and 1975, an epic win over the Soviet Red Army team, and key games in the remarkable 35-game unbeaten streak in 1979–80. And who could ever forget our Cinderella run to get to the 2010 Finals?

But it hasn't been all glitz and glamour.

When the Flyers franchise was awarded, Ed Snider and Jerry Wolman were taking a huge risk. You see, I was in the minority—a die-hard hockey fan who had followed the old Philadelphia Ramblers, who played at the Philadelphia Arena in the Eastern Hockey League. At that time, however, most Philadelphians knew little about hockey.

Across the bridge at the Cherry Hill Arena, the Jersey Devils were playing in the Eastern Hockey League. They were the lone survivors of seven failed Philadelphia-area, minor-league teams over a 38-year period.

But in 1966 (a year before we started playing), Philly landed a franchise at a cost of $2 million, in part because of plans to build a new rink, the Spectrum. That helped offset the fact that Philadelphia was the only one of six new NHL franchises not to have a high minor-league affiliation.

The team was named "Flyers" by Ed Snider's sister, Phyllis. That was the easy part. The tough part: attracting fans in a city with deep baseball, football, and basketball roots. In addition, several months of hockey's shedule overlapped with the immensely popular Big Five basketball scene.

In 1967, a parade to welcome the team was held down Broad Street. About 25 people showed up. As defenseman Joe Watson is fond of saying, there were more Flyers personnel *in* the parade than there were people watching it.

Today, virtually all home games are sellouts and the Flyers have become a huge part of Philadelphia's sports landscape. But in 1967–68, there were growing pains. Lots and lots of growing pains. We lost our first exhibition game 6–1—to a minor-league team. Well, at least it was *our* minor-league team, the Quebec Aces.

The regular-season home opener drew 7,812 fans, and we eked out a less-than-artistic 1–0 win over the Pittsburgh Penguins as Bill

Sutherland scored the goal, Doug Favell recorded the shutout, and public-address announcer Gene Hart kept the spectators informed as he explained the icing and offside calls. I announced the goal scorers and penalties to those who sat in our scarcely filled press box. Today, in the Information Age, there may be 50 to 75 media types at our games. Back then, you could count the reporters on one hand.

I also kept handwritten stats during the season—remember, this was *way* before computers—and handed them out to reporters after the game. My Catholic school penmanship, drilled into me by the nuns, was actually paying off.

I got the job, which was part-time, partly because of my friendship with Joe Kadlec. Joe had been working for the *Daily News* sports department and was hired as the Flyers' first public-relations director. I had met Joe the previous year down in Margate, New Jersey. We were young, single, and carefree, and we partied and chased women together.

To be honest, I found out about the Flyers because of a big billboard on Route 42 in South Jersey that read, THE FLYERS ARE COMING! I looked into it because I had a little bit of a background in hockey. The goal judge for the Ramblers—a team that was here from 1955 to 1964—was a guy named George Lennon. George was the uncle of a classmate of mine in grade school, also named George Lennon. We used to go to the games with his uncle on Friday nights at the arena on 45th and Market. We'd watch the games and run around the rink. We'd get the broken sticks, take them home, and tape them up and play street hockey behind the school. We did that for years. We'd put on our shoe-skates—you put the skates on your shoes—and we'd play all the time.

As I mentioned, I was a rarity at that time. I was hooked on hockey even though we didn't have our own NHL team. I lived in

4

a Southwest Philadelphia row home at the time, and I'd take the 36 Trolley downtown to buy hockey books. I'd watch the Original Six teams—Montreal, Boston, Toronto, Detroit, Chicago, and the New York Rangers—on TV and I just loved the sport. I got to know the league and read all the hockey books, which they only sold at 13th and Market. And then one day when I was talking to Joe, he told me he just got the job with the Flyers as the PR director. I said, "Hey, if you need any help, I'd be glad to help you. I know a little bit about the sport." Joe told me to come to this cocktail party where they were celebrating the team's arrival. Joe was a North Catholic guy and I was a West Catholic guy, but we became buddies down Margate through some mutual friends.

It's strange how your life can take a turn by fate. I'm sure everybody can look back to an unscripted event that changed their lives in some way. For me, if it wasn't for some friends bringing Joe and me together, I probably would never have been a part of the Flyers.

As it turned out, we had two press boxes at the Spectrum, and Joe used me to handle one of them. I handed out stats and did a lot of the early work that Ted Gendron, Don Schwartz, Gene Prince, and a few others did in later years. I would announce the goals over the press box PA, but I missed lots and lots of goals as they were being scored while I was busy writing down things on a sheet of paper. I'd be printing something out and there would be a big roar and I'd find out what happened and then make the announcement.

I did that for a few years. Gene Hart—who, of course, would become a legendary announcer and would be named to Hockey's Hall of Fame—was one of a series of guys who did the early public address announcing in the arena, and he would then do the third period on the radio. Marv Bachrad, Eddie Ferenz, and Kevin Johnson also did some PA work.

With Hall of Fame broadcaster Gene Hart (right).

The first season started positively enough. We finished that 1967–68 campaign atop the newly formed West Division, which was also composed of teams in Pittsburgh, St. Louis (our most bitter rival back then), Minnesota, Los Angeles, and Oakland.

Looking back, it wasn't that we were very good. We just weren't as bad as the other teams. We won the West but had just a 31–32–11 record, a .493 points percentage.

The competition level was in two totally different levels in our first season. You had the Original Six in one division—and you had very little chance to beat them unless something happened and they took you lightly—and the expansion teams in the other division.

We had just two 20-goal scorers that first year: Leon Rochefort (21) and Sutherland (20). Lou Angotti, who was the first captain in club history, was another veteran, and he led the team with 49 points. Overall, I think our scouting guys did a great job with the expansion draft and picked a nice mix of experienced players and those who were up and coming. Interestingly, we had four regulars on that first team who, seven years later, played a vital part in winning the Stanley Cup: Gary Dornhoefer, Joe Watson, Eddie Van Impe, and Bernie Parent. Joe and Dorny were just 24 in our first season, and Eddie was 27. Bernie was just 22, and his best years were ahead of him. Hall of Fame years, I might add.

Eddie was the classic stay-at-home defenseman. Rock-solid on the ice and a prankster off it—a guy who would put sneezing powder on your shoulder if you weren't looking and cut your ties in half. He and Garry Peters, another guy we selected in the expansion draft, kept the guys loose.

So when you look at it, the Flyers got one-third of their 1974 championship defense (Watson and Van Impe) from the expansion draft, along with a sensational goalie (Parent, who was traded and then brought back) and very good scorer (Dornhoefer). That's pretty good scouting! Give props to general manager Bud Poile and coach Keith Allen—each of whom were hired from Western Hockey League teams—and super scout Marcel Pelletier.

In the expansion draft, each team got to select 18 skaters and two goalies. The Original Six teams were permitted to protect 11 players and one goalie. For the first two picks, they were allowed to protect an additional player after one was selected. Anyone who had not completed two full pro seasons was exempt from the draft.

In the goalie portion of the draft, the Flyers selected the 22-year-old Parent from the Boston Bruins, which surprised many because there were several notable veterans available, including Glenn Hall and Ed Johnston. The Flyers later picked Favell, also from the Bruins, as Parent's backup. Smart picks, it turned out. Bernie was 16–17–5 with a 2.48 goals-against average in our first year, and Favy went 15–15–6 with a 2.27 goals-against average. Like Steve Mason and Michal Neuvirth in 2015–16, Parent and Favell provided solid goaltending for the majority of our first season. And the nice part was that both were 22 when we drafted them, so both appeared to have bright futures.

Little did we know that one of them would become one of the most popular athletes in Philadelphia sports history and would eventually cause a bumper sticker to be plastered on seemingly every other car in the Delaware Valley: ONLY THE LORD SAVES MORE THAN BERNIE PARENT.

Hearing from the Boss

I would see our owner, Ed Snider, in locker rooms after games in our first year. That was a tradition that started in 1967 and continued until he passed away in 2016. He always loved being around the players, loved getting to know them and finding out about their families and their lives. Ed wasn't just some corporate guy whom the players never saw. The franchise was his baby and he was totally immersed in it, and it showed in his deep respect and admiration for the players. Back in our first year, I would see the guys from the group who ran the team—Ed, Joe Scott, and Bill Putnam. They were all excited about making the Flyers become a big part of Philadelphia.

I always called Ed by his first name, but to some—like Bob Clarke—he was always *Mr. Snider.* And when I got the PA job, Ed would call me on my phone in the box if things got really strange down on the ice. He never called me if he agreed with a call, but he'd call me if he wanted a clarification on something that happened. A lot. He might ask me why one of his players was getting a penalty or what it looked like from my level on the ice. I would say, "I don't quite understand it, Ed. I know what you mean." But I would never say that to the referee. I had to stay professional with the ref.

I remember one game when there was a huge brawl, and Bob Myers was the ref. He came over to me and started telling me all the penalties he was handing out so I could announce them. This went on for a while because there were a lot of penalties. Just then, the phone rang and it was Ed. I said, "Just a minute, Ed," and I put the phone down because Myers wanted to finish up. When Myers finished, I got back on the phone with Ed. He said, "Lou, there's something you and I have to get straight between us." I said, "Sure, Ed, what's that?" And he said, "When I call you, I want the referee put on hold." That was Ed. He just wanted to blow off some steam. Everybody used to kid me that I was on his speed dial from his suite.

There wasn't much Ed missed. A couple years ago, I was introducing the Mites-on-Ice before they took the ice between periods of our game. Somebody handed me a piece of paper with the kids' names and I announced them as they skate out. Well, I announced a couple of kids and said they were from a certain playground in the area—but it turned out they were from the Ed Snider Youth Hockey Foundation. That immediately sparked a phone call from Ed. He said, "Where did you get that information?" He just wanted to know whose responsibility it was and we quickly settled it. Ed wanted the foundation to be credited—and they deserved it because they are a fantastic organization. But that was Ed. He was involved in every aspect and he was so excited about the foundation and took so much pride in it.

* * *

Back in our first year, it was fun to see the young and old guys try to blend together. During training camp, Keith Allen, our coach, issued what he called his 10 commandments. Among them: players weren't permitted to go to local taverns, and they were told to curb their use of profanity on the ice and not to break sticks in fits of anger. I'm not sure how many "commandments" were broken.

I remember being on a couple of charter flights and going to some road games in that first season, including our first matchup in Montreal. I sat in the press box, did stats, and accommodated our beat writers if they had any questions.

Now, remember; Montreal was the Mecca of the hockey world—like the Yankees were to baseball back then.

In just our ninth game of our first season, we went into Montreal on November 4. This was only our second game against an established team, and we were obviously heavy underdogs. None of the established teams wanted to lose to one of the new guys because, quite frankly, it would be a big embarrassment. Especially at home.

But there we are, in the hallowed Forum, taking the lead against the mighty Habs. Bernie Parent and Leon Rochefort were playing out of their minds. Bernie was from Montreal, and Rochefort had been drafted from the Canadiens, so both had extra incentive, and we took a 2–1 lead going into the third period. Rochefort scored two goals in the third period to complete his hat trick and give us a 4–1 lead against Rogie Vachon, the Canadiens goalie who would later go into the Hall of Fame.

As Al Michaels would later ask, "Do you believe in miracles?"

In the press box, John Brogan, the Flyers beat writer for the *Bulletin*, gave me an assignment. There were about five minutes left in the game and I guess he was on deadline and didn't have time to go downstairs for postgame interviews and file his story on time, so he asked me to grab him a couple of quotes from Allen, our coach.

I must preface what happened next. I was not a newspaper reporter and, at that time, I had had no idea about the protocol for interviewing the coach or the players. So I went down the steps, ran through a corridor, and worked my way to the Flyers' bench and walked right up to Keith Allen with about two minutes to go. Keith is in the middle of trying to coach his team to a monumental victory, and I say, "Keith, can I talk to you for a minute?"

Keith replied with a simple question. "What the hell are you doing here?"

"John Brogan sent me down to get a couple quotes from you."

Keith was flabbergasted. He shooed me away in a polite way. Sort of. "Tell him I'm really happy that things are going well for us. Now get the hell out of here!" And as he's talking to me, he's yelling to his players and making a line change. It was pure naiveté on my part.

Later, Brogan tells me he was up in the press box watching me talk to Keith and he's shaking his head in disbelief. But I didn't know any different. I didn't know I was supposed to wait until the game was *finished* and talk to him in the locker room. Afterward, Keith saw me in the locker room and said, "Lou, if we would have lost that game, you were walking back to Philadelphia."

But Keith was a classy guy. He was smiling after the game, but I'm just glad we didn't blow the lead.

We actually started out very well against the so-called established teams, going a stunning 4–1–1 in our first five games against them. Then reality set in. We lost our next eight to the Original Six and when the year ended, we were just 8–15–1 against the East, but a healthy 23–17–10 against the expansion West.

When Las Vegas joined the league in 2017–18, the drafting rules made it easier for it to field a competitive team right away. Then again, Vegas won't have the luxury of playing most of its games against expansion teams like the West did in 1967–68.

One thing that's almost certain: Vegas won't have to play any of its "home" games on the road, like we did in that crazy first season. We played seven "home" games away from the Spectrum because portions of the roof came crashing down on February 17, 1968, as fans were getting ready to watch the Ice Capades.

The roof was fixed a few days later. But less than two weeks after it was supposedly repaired, more roof problems surfaced and the Spectrum was closed indefinitely.

We ended up playing a so-called home game in Madison Square Garden in New York, another in Maple Leaf Gardens in Toronto, and five in Quebec City, which was the home of the Quebec Aces, our minor league team at the time. We went 3–2–2 in those games, so we picked up points in five of the seven games—a pretty good accomplishment. You might even call it *Rocky*-esque. During one late-season stretch, we played seven straight games—and 14 of our last 17—away from the Spectrum. I think the guys rallied around the fact that they were going to be road warriors, so to speak, for a long time.

But fixing the roof became a big political issue. In the *Bulletin*, Sandy Grady wrote: "Philadelphia's $12 million toy is busted and there are no grownups to fix it. Instead, there are 50-year-old children throwing temper tantrums, blaming each other for breaking it, and claiming that it was a lousy toy anyway."

Despite all the traveling and the hardship and inconvenience that went with it, we somehow survived and won the West title. The roof was repaired in time for the playoffs against St. Louis, but we lost in a seven-game series—with the clinching Game 7 at the Spectrum.

Maybe if we would have played that last game at a neutral site like, say, Toronto, we would have won. Who knows? After the roof problem, the players seemed to take playing on the road in stride. I think a lot of those guys were just happy to be playing in the NHL at all, and they handled it very professionally. If it would have happened in the beginning of the year, I think it would have been handled differently than it was toward the end of the season. By the time the roof came off, the players had gotten to know each other and had found a comfort level on the ice together. Flyers teams have always had good bonds, and that first team kind of led the way. I think that team also bonded because of things that happened on the ice, especially some of the nasty brawls we had with St. Louis. I think that brought our guys together. The Blues pushed us around a bit, but Ed Snider took care of that and we soon added some tough guys of our own.

That first team didn't have an overabundance of talent, but it had grit and heart—and, in a way, set the tone for the franchise's identity. When you think of the Flyers, the first players that pop into your mind are probably Bobby Clarke, Bernie Parent, Bill Barber, and Eric Lindros. Rightfully so. But there's something to be said about guys such as Leon Rochefort, Bill Sutherland, Lou Angotti, and Gary Dornhoefer. They were pioneers of sorts and they got this franchise off to a proud start.

People ask me to compare the level of play of the early Flyers to today, and that's difficult because the game is so much different now. I think there are exceptional talents now, just like you had back then. The early Flyers teams had as much tenacity and desire as the guys in the 21st century. But they don't come close to matching the speed and preparation that we see today. How many players took the puck and wound their way up the ice back then? Not many. I think players are much better coached now and much more aware of nutrition and doing the right things off the ice. They get better coaching at a young age now and they develop quicker. They come into training camp ready to go. Back then, training camp was used to work your way into shape. Now, if you don't arrive at camp in shape, you're in trouble, because someone will take your job.

The other big difference is bigger goalie equipment. Because of that, games are still low-scoring—even though most forwards are more gifted than in the expansion days and the first few decades that followed. When you go back to the days of Bernie Parent and Terry Sawchuk, you can appreciate just how good they were when you see that their catching mitts looked like one you would use at first base, and they didn't have as big of a pad on the back of the other one. Now they're so *gigantic*.

There are a lot of subtle differences in watching the game, too. I was recently looking at an old replay—back in the days when I had black hair and was a lot thinner—and it really struck me that the walls around the rink were bare. Totally white—like my hair now. Now you see advertisements everywhere.

When I'm at a game at the Wells Fargo Center today, I appreciate the big crowds, because I can remember when the Spectrum was half-full in the early days. I give credit to the people who sold the game to Philadelphia back then—people like Ed Snider, Joe Scott, Lou Scheinfeld, and Gene Hart. It was a rough-and-tumble city and it wasn't as if this team was going to come in and immediately have people latch on to them. I often think about what Gene Hart did for this franchise. People loved Gene because he actually explained everything in his broadcasts—and he didn't make anybody feel like he was talking down to them. He always did it in a professional manner.

He explained it in a way that you could grasp it. I think most people understand that the team owes a lot to Gene for what he did.

As for the crowds, I think they're different now. In the early days, you saw the same people at all the games. Behind me I had low glass, and I'd see the same folks in the seats every night. They all became my friends. They'd bring me birthday cakes and things. But it was the same people. Now I don't see the same people at games. I think maybe groups of people divide tickets up and you see different people at the games.

The first year at the Spectrum, tickets were $2 to $5. It was a cozy place, and the fans were right on top of the action. The Wells Fargo Center also has great sight lines, and I feel very privileged to have worked in both buildings. There are so many great memories. The two Cups at the Spectrum stand out, but we've had some unbelievable moments at the Wells Fargo Center, too. The Eric Lindros / John LeClair years were very special. And who can forget our miracle run in 2010? We got into the playoffs with a shootout win on the last day of the regular season and then ended up going all the way to the Stanley Cup Finals before losing on a goal that not many people ever saw. Claude Giroux is the only player from that team who is still here, but I get the sense that this team is headed toward some very special times.

You see the young guys like Shayne Gostisbehere working their way into the lineup and making a major impact, and the farm system is as good as it's been in a long, long time. I really feel like this team is on the verge of turning the corner.

The current team is a close-knit group. That seems to be a common thread through the 50 years this franchise has been around. Each team develops its own identity, and it seems there's always a guy or two who keeps everyone loose, whether it's a Chris Pronger or a Scott Hartnell or a Michael Del Zotto.

Fans would bring me a cake each year and present it to me in the Spectrum penalty box on or near my birthday on December 3. To the left is NHL official Charlie Roeser, while off-ice official Tom Coyle is on the right.

Back in our early years, one of those guys was Ed Van Impe. During one road trip, I remember we were going from New York to Toronto, and again, John Brogan of the *Bulletin* is in the middle of this story. The players used to pull a lot of pratical jokes. John was on the plane reading *GQ* magazine. Now, John was not someone who seemed like he was into fashion, so it was interesting that he was reading this. But he was thumbing through the pages, and he saw that the shoes he's wearing were featured in the magazine. He was so excited that he took off his shoe and passed it over to me while we were sitting on the plane. I said, "Pretty nice." And Ed Van Impe, who was sitting behind me, asked to see it.

It was the last John saw of his shoe for a long time, and he was not happy about it.

We got to Toronto and it was snowing and sleeting. Very, very nasty weather. And John came up the ramp wearing one shoe—the kind featured in *GQ*—and one of his galoshes. The galoshes, I think it's fair to say, were not in *GQ*. That shoe disappeared on that trip. But one day, some of the players had a coffee can full of concrete. It had a small hockey stick that was sticking out of it—with John's shoe attached to the stick. The players presented it to John as a trophy. This was probably a year after it mysteriously disappeared.

John was a good sport about it and always a lot of fun. Years later, he ended up working for the Flyers.

There was a lot of that kind of stuff on the road. Sometimes they would get behind you and cut your hair if you were asleep on the plane. I remember one year they wanted to cut my hair, but I'm told Dick Cherry saved me. Dick was the brother of Don Cherry, who used to coach the Bruins but became famous for his loud jackets and his loud comments on *Hockey Night in Canada*. Dick was the opposite of his brother—very laid-back, very classy.

And because of him, I never got an unwanted haircut.

CHAPTER 2

THE FRANCHISE
TURNS THE CORNER

After they joined the league, the Flyers had five straight losing seasons, though we were pretty good at tying opponents, with 87 ties in five seasons. (Remember ties?)

And then the Flyers hired me as their public address announcer, and we started our ascent toward becoming a Stanley Cup contender.

I'm smiling as I write this, of course, because the *real* reason the Flyers began their climb in 1972–73 was because Bobby Clarke blossomed into a superstar, Rick MacLeish had a breakout season, and Bill Barber emerged as one of the NHL's best rookies.

Oh, and it didn't hurt that Bill "Cowboy" Flett erupted for 43 goals in 1972–73, or that Gary Dornhoefer (30 goals) had a career season.

By the end of our season, you could tell that something special was being built here.

I moved down from the press box to become the Spectrum's public address announcer in 1972–73 because Kevin Johnson left to become the public relations director with the Philadelphia Blazers of the World Hockey Association. My new seat was at ice level between the two penalty boxes, and, oh, the stories I can tell—and will, as this book progresses.

To get the public address announcer's job, I had to audition for Lou Scheinfeld, who was the Flyers vice president. The audition was set up during the installation of the third deck in the Spectrum in the summer. I put a microphone on and there were cranes moving around and the building was really noisy. Over the microphone, I half-kidded with the construction workers. I told them, "Guys, excuse me. I've got an important audition here. Can you turn off the cranes?" Surprisingly, they listened and turned them off. And just then, Lou said, "That's all right. If these cranes don't bother you, nothing will. I know you have the voice for it." And that's how my new career started.

I quickly learned that I had to pay attention at all times because I might have a puck, a stick, or a player in my lap. Or even a bucket of ice. We worked without glass back then, so it could get dangerous. There was nothing between me and the players in the penalty box and no glass in front of us. The first game I did was in the preseason, and a player from Minnesota—I think it might have been Dennis O'Brien—picked up a bucket that was filled with pucks and ice chips in his penalty box and threw it at Bob Kelly in the other penalty box. The referee quickly calmed things down before an all-out brawl started, which wasn't uncommon back in those days.

Lots of interesting stuff has happened next to me in those penalty boxes. Lots of things that seem right out of the movie *Slap Shot*. For me, the Hanson Brothers were played by guys named Schultz, Plager, and Domi, among countless others.

* * *

Many people say the Flyers became woven into the city's fabric when Robert Earl Clarke came aboard in 1969–70. Clarke was gritty, like the hardworking, blue-collar people in this city. But he was also quiet, soft-spoken, and oh so humble. On the ice, however, he didn't back down from anyone. If two players went into the corner for a puck, odds were that No. 16 would come out with possession.

Slowly, the Flyers began surrounding Clarke with missing pieces. Much like current general manager Ron Hextall is trying to do now around his captain, Claude Giroux.

In Clarke's rookie season, the Flyers finished a dismal 17–35–24. Yes, 24 ties. As a side note, I never had any ill feelings about ties.

Both teams came out with a point, usually well-deserved, and both felt like they had accomplished something. Flip the calendar to today and we have a freak show called a shootout. I never liked them. Never will. It just doesn't seem right when a team that had the better territorial play in regulation and overtime loses in a fluky shootout. It feels gimmicky and dirty. Almost Roller Derby-ish.

But I digress.

Back to Clarkie. I remember going to training camp in Quebec City and he was on a line with Reggie Fleming and Lew Morrison, and they just set the camp on fire. That's why Lewie made the team. Reggie was a protector of Clarkie, and Clarkie never stopped on the ice. Never took a game off. Never took a shift off. Never had a big celebration after he scored. He'd score a goal and the stick was down. He rarely celebrated—except when it was an important one, like the big overtime goal he scored to win Game 2 in Boston when we won our first Cup. There was no looking back on him. He just kept getting better and better, and he was the ultimate team guy, the ultimate leader, the ultimate agitator.

Clarkie never talked about being diabetic, but I think that motivated him. He slipped down to the second round of the 1969 amateur draft because teams questioned whether his body could withstand a full NHL season. I think teams envisioned he would break down because of his condition, and I always got the feeling he wanted to prove those teams wrong.

And I think his teammates respected him even more because of what he had to overcome. Here's a guy giving himself needles and with a tough medical condition, and he's outworking everybody on the ice every night. How could that not serve as a motivator to everyone else?

I remember one night we were on a train in Montreal and heading to Toronto for a game, and there was a mix-up with the food and it went to the Montreal players—they were on the train car next to ours—and Joe Watson was all upset because he knew Clarkie couldn't go long without food because of his condition. I can still hear him saying, "We need to get Clarkie something to eat!" He was very caring toward Clarkie, because he was his teammate and he would do anything for him, but he also knew he was his meal ticket.

We weren't the toughest of teams when Clarkie first broke into the league, but by his fourth season, we didn't get pushed around because three of our hard-nosed draft picks—Bob Kelly, Dave Schultz, and Don Saleski—were in the lineup. Teams liked to take runs at Clarkie, but with Kelly, Schultz, and Saleski around, that didn't happen much because they knew they would have to pay a price.

When Clarkie started his fourth year in the league, I took over the public address duties. By then, I had given up taking night college classes at St. Joseph's, where I was studying business and marketing. This thing called hockey got in the way of my education, but I never regretted it.

Clarke's fourth season was spectacular. Playing with Flett on his right side and, for part of the year, with Barber on his left, he erupted for 104 points and was named the league's MVP, beating out players like Phil Esposito, Bobby Orr, Ken Dryden, and Gilbert Perreault. MacLeish, then 23 years old, became the youngest player in the league's history to score 50 goals in a season. So you had a 37-goal, 67-assist player centering the first line, and a 50-goal, 50-assist player centering the second line. To use a baseball analogy, it was a one-two punch like Mays–McCovey in the 1960s, or Trout–Pujols in the 2010s.

We finished second in the West that season with a 37–30–11 record. Nothing spectacular, but an aura was starting to develop around this team. That aura grew in the playoffs. First, we beat Minnesota in the opening round—our first playoff series win in franchise history—and we headed to Montreal to face the heavily favored Canadiens.

Younger fans may not realize it, but the statue of Gary Dornhoefer that stands near our arena was created because of that series against the Minnesota North Stars. The series was tied at two wins apiece and we were getting outplayed in the overtime when, suddenly, Dorny weaved through the North Stars' defense and beat goaltender Cesare Maniago on a breakaway. We then won the series in Game 6.

Dorny's goal was later immortalized in a statue, showing him leaping into the air after his gorgeous move produced the game-winning score. It was a fitting tribute because, to me, he was one of the most unheralded Flyers of that era. He was an original Flyer and he would station himself in front of the net and absorb lots of punishment—much like Tim Kerr and Wayne Simmonds in later years—because he wanted to be in position for a loose puck. I don't remember the phrase "dirty goals" being mentioned back then like it is today, but that area in front of the net was Dorny's office. He set up camp there and was tough to move—and he scored a ton of dirty goals from that spot.

His goal keyed the playoff win over the North Stars, who many considered to be the favorite in that series. Minnesota had a more veteran team and a lot of firepower, including guys like Dennis Hextall (the uncle of Ron Hextall, the Flyers' current general manager), Jude Drouin, and Danny Grant.

So we went to Montreal in the Stanley Cup semifinals and ended up losing in five games, but that is very misleading. We actually came close to taking control of the series. In Montreal.

We stunned the Habs in the opener in overtime 5–4 and came close to taking a 2–0 lead in the series before losing 4–3, also in overtime, in Game 2. Then we lost three straight hard-fought games, and our season was over. But you could feel a sense of confidence building, and you couldn't wait for the next season to begin. This team had lots of talent and lots of toughness, and Keith Allen—who was then the general manager—made one of the most important trades in franchise history shortly after that season ended, bringing back Bernie Parent in a trade with Toronto. Bernie had been dealt to the Maple Leafs two years earlier, and his return was greeted with open arms by the players. He was a popular player with the fans and in the locker room, and he was just reaching the prime of his career.

Before too long, his trademark line—"We're having some fun, eh?"—would become famous to Flyers fans.

Sanders Not Philly's Most Popular Bernie

When the Democratic National Convention was held at the Wells Fargo Center in the summer of 2016—Hillary Clinton watched her daughter, Chelsea, make her speech on a TV in the visitors' locker room—chants of "Ber-nie, Ber-nie, Ber-nie" filled the air as a salute to Bernie Sanders, the Vermont senator.

Once upon a time, those same chants were heard time and again at the old Spectrum in honor of Bernie Parent. They were part of the fans' battle cry during our Stanley Cup championship runs of 1974 and 1975.

Funny thing is, Bernie almost didn't get a chance to lead us to the Promised Land.

Midway through the 1970–71 season, Bernie was called into general manager Keith Allen's office. Keith had moved from coach to GM and he was about to drop a bombshell: Bernie had been dealt to Toronto.

Keith told Parent it was the most difficult trade he had ever made, but that didn't ease the goalie's pain. One of the most popular players with his teammates and the fans, Bernie was floored and he began sobbing. He thought he had found a home in Philadelphia.

In the book *Bernie Parent Unmasked*, Bernie writes that he "cried like a baby" when he got the news. "I bumped into Mr. Snider in the corridor at the Spectrum and he started crying, too."

Bernie was totally stunned. Getting traded like that disrupts your whole life. You're playing well and then, *boom*, you're gone.

Parent and a 1971 second-round draft pick went to Toronto for center Mike Walton, goalie Bruce Gamble, and a first-round pick that year. The three-way trade also had the Flyers sending Walton to Boston for center/winger MacLeish and right winger Danny Schock.

Trading Bernie surprised a lot of us. Walton was a pretty good scorer at the time and we needed scoring, but he never came here. I remember thinking, "Who's this guy MacLeish?"

The trade made the less-consistent Doug Favell the No. 1 goalie. Dealing Bernie, however, didn't sit well with the fans. They thought the wrong goalie had been dealt. Everyone loved Bernie. One sign at the Spectrum read: JUDAS, BENEDICT ARNOLD, AND NOW KEITH ALLEN.

In Bernie's one-and-a-half years in Toronto, he got to play—and learn—alongside his idol, Jacques Plante, who helped fine-tune Parent's game.

After the 1971–72 season, Bernie got into a contract dispute with Toronto and jumped to the Philadelphia Blazers of the fledging World Hockey Association. He was in the right city, but the wrong team. That would soon change after he got into a contract squabble with the Blazers. He left the team after the first game of the playoffs and became a free agent.

Bernie had been the first NHL player to jump to the World Hockey Association, but he wanted to return to our league. He said he was being pursued by New York in the WHA, but decided to take a pay cut to come back to the Flyers.

"I want to play in Philadelphia," he said at the time.

Remember how I talked about how an unexpected event can change your life? For me, it was meeting Joe Kadlec, who steered me toward a 50-year (and counting) tenure with the Flyers.

For Bernie, it was a salary dispute with Toronto—and then the Blazers—and the ramifications that followed.

If Bernie had signed with the Maple Leafs, he may have had a long and prosperous career in Toronto...and we might still be searching for our first Stanley Cup. His contract squabble in Toronto indirectly changed the fortunes of our franchise.

Before the 1973–74 season—when we won our first Cup—Keith Allen brought Bernie back by dealing Favell and a first-round draft pick to Toronto. We received Bernie and a second-round draft pick. Even though Bernie had played for the Blazers, Toronto still owned his NHL rights.

After the trade, Favy, who used to be Bernie's roommate, had a couple of less-than-spectacular seasons with the Maple Leafs and then finished his NHL career with the Colorado Rockies before having a curtain call with the Philadelphia Firebirds in the AHL. (I saw

Favy at one of our 50-year celebrations in 2017, and he looked great. Still had the gift of gab and a ton of one-liners.)

And Bernie? He played in a staggering 73 games for us in his first year back and he blossomed into one of the best goalies in NHL history. And, so, yes, Keith Allen was vindicated—and in addition to getting a world-class goalie, he got a scoring machine as a bonus, Ricky MacLeish.

I guess that's why they called him "Keith the Thief."

Is Hexy Another Keith Allen?

I think when you talk about "bests" in Flyers history, Keith Allen would have to be the franchise's top general manager. Hands down. He had the ability to recognize when it was best to make a big deal, and he was an expert at dealing a guy just before he reached a downturn in his career.

Keith coached that ragtag group that was our first team, and after he moved up to general manager, he just had a way about him. He was a very classy man and, because he had been around the league for a while, he got to know everybody. He was a very experienced guy. It wasn't like he was coming in brand new like, say, Russ Farwell, who became our general manager in 1990 but never had any NHL experience as a player, coach, or executive.

I see a little bit of Keith in Ron Hextall, our current general manager.

Keith made some daring moves, but, for the most part, he built through the draft and with young guys he acquired in trades.

Hexy is trying to follow a similar path.

Of course, there's a big change in the way general managers have to operate today because of the salary cap, which wasn't around during Keith's days here. Not that the players made a lot of money back then, but if there was somebody Keith wanted—or, years later, when Clarkie or Paul Holmgren were the GMs—Ed Snider would open up his checkbook.

In a way, it's much tougher to be a general manager in today's cap world. To win a Stanley Cup, not only do you have to put together a great 20-man roster, but it has to be a very *balanced* roster in terms of salaries handed out. That can be very tricky. Some teams put all their eggs in one basket—they have four or five very high-priced players and then spread out the other salaries with lower contracts. Some general managers only have a couple of high-priced players and try to have more "even" salaries throughout the team.

There's no exact science. No right way and no wrong way. Everybody has their own style, and a lot of it depends on how many young guys you have who are impact players right away—when their salaries aren't as high.

I'm a finance guy. That's what I do for a living. I worked for a bank and now I sell securities to banks, so I'm fascinated by the way general managers handle the cap and how they allocate different percentages of the cap to their goalies, defensemen, and forwards. I'm fascinated that some people can make it work, and some can't make it work. As I said, there's no right way and no wrong way, but there's a lot of consternation that goes into the player-personnel decisions. Look at Chicago after they beat us to win the Stanley Cup in 2010. They had to unload a lot of salary and make deals because contracts were coming up and they couldn't keep everybody. So they got rid of some key players, including Dustin Byfuglien, Andrew Ladd, and Antti Niemi, and started the process again. It was almost like a purge. And, lo and behold, they won Cups again in 2013 and 2015. Give Chicago general manager Stan Bowman a lot of credit for the way he was able to navigate the system and produce what has to be considered a dynasty in today's cap world.

With Chicago, they have gotten rid of some very talented players and you wonder, "How are they going to replace that guy?" Well, they do. They don't seem to skip a beat.

It's a lot more difficult to produce powerhouses in today's NHL like Montreal, the New York Islanders, and Edmonton Oilers did back in the day. Yet, somehow, Chicago was able to do that. The key was their strong foundation of young players and drafting players like Patrick Kane, Jonathan Toews, Duncan Keith, and Corey Crawford.

I think that's the plan Hexy has in place here. You look at guys he's drafted like Ivan Provorov, Travis Konecny, Travis Sanheim, Oskar Lindblom, and Carter Hart, among others, and you can see a strong foundation in place. He did a great job of clearing out some contracts in his first couple years as general manager, and that wasn't easy to do.

If he can continue to add quality prospects and lop off what's at the other end—the guys with the big contracts who aren't producing—he's going to build a winner.

I think the fans have bought into Hexy. They're filling the building, which is great, and they understand what he's doing. They see he has a plan and that it's going to take some time, but in the long run, it's going to succeed. Now, I know there are some fans out there that wanted Hexy to go after Steven Stamkos before he re-signed with Tampa Bay in 2016. But the bottom line is, he *couldn't* go after a Steven Stamkos in a salary-cap world.

The Bombshell GM

Paul Holmgren was the general manager before Hexy, and he shook the franchise's foundation with two trades 30 minutes apart in the summer of 2011. I can't think of a more shocking set of moves in our history.

First he traded Jeff Carter, who had averaged 38 goals per year in his previous three seasons, to Columbus for Jake Voracek and two draft picks—a first-rounder than turned out to be Sean Couturier, and a third-rounder that turned out to be Nick Cousins.

He then dealt Mike Richards, the team's captain, to Los Angeles for Wayne Simmonds, Brayden Schenn, and a second-round draft pick that was later included in a trade for Nick Grossmann, a big defenseman from Dallas.

Richards and Carter both had lengthy contracts and they were the faces of our franchise. When I think of that day, I'm still stunned that it happened.

As it turned out, Homer made shrewd moves. We ended up with two wingers who turned into all-stars, Voracek and Simmonds; a consistent scorer in Schenn; and one of the NHL's best defensive forwards, Couturier. So you'd have to say we came out ahead.

I knew there were all kinds of rumors out there that Richie and Carter liked to go out and party and all this kind of stuff. But, I mean, they're millionaire young kids living downtown. What are they gonna do, become hermits? They can't do that; it's bad for you.

As for their lifestyles, it's never as much as people say it is, or as little as people say it is. It's probably somewhere in the middle.

But I was really surprised when the trades came down. I was sitting by my computer in my home office and my son, Jeff, came into the room and told me we had traded Carter. I said, "Get out of here." I was stunned, but I could see right away it was true. It was all over the Internet. And then I got busy with work and I was in the middle of a phone call when he came busting in again and told me Richards got traded. I said, "What? Come on!" And sure enough, he was right.

I've been around the game for a half century, so I know that anybody can be traded at any time. But to have both guys traded? Within a half hour of each other?! I was floored, because there had been a long-term commitment to both guys.

Homer said he wanted to get bigger up front, especially on the wings, which is why he wanted Simmonds and Voracek. He called Schenn a "diamond in the rough" and said he was "probably the best young player outside the NHL."

As for Richie and Carts, I always thought they were a little distant. I guess they wanted their privacy and kind of kept people at arm's length. But that was just their personalities, and I never really thought much about it. They both had some very productive years here.

Richards had some off-ice problems and was out of hockey in 2016–17. Carter, of course, later ended up with the Kings, and he has a shot to land in the Hall of Fame someday. Both have two Stanley Cup rings, so it worked out for them, too.

The day we traded the two players, Holmgren praised their contributions and said they were "extremely upset." He said the calls were "tough for me to make and tough for them to receive."

After the trades, we suddenly had about $13 million in cap space, and we promptly signed colorful free-agent goalie Ilya Bryzgalov to a nine-year, $51 million contract.

It would be the beginning of the end for Sergei Bobrovsky's Flyers career. Bobrovsky served as Bryz's backup for a year but wanted to go someplace where he could become the starter. He was traded to Columbus the next season for three draft picks that turned out to be goalie Anthony Stolarz, left winger Taylor Leier, and a fourth-round 2013 selection that we sent to the Kings for Simon Gagne.

In hindsight, the worst part of bombshell Carter/Richards deals was that they indirectly led to us trading a young goaltender who would become a Vezina Trophy winner and an all-star.

The Forgotten GM

To me, the most underrated general manager in our history is Bud Poile. He was our first GM, and he did a great job with the expansion draft and setting the franchise's foundation.

He was here only two seasons, but his fingerprints are all over the franchise.

Poile, who died in 2005 at age 80, had a big hand in bringing Bernie Parent and Bobby Clarke to Philadelphia. The rest, as they say, is history. Clarke and Parent are regarded as the best two players to ever wear the Orange and Black.

The expansion draft included four players—Parent, Ed Van Impe, Joe Watson, and Dornhoefer—who were key during our Stanley Cup seasons. And Poile's 1969 draft included Clarke (second round), Schultz (fifth round), and Saleski (sixth round), forwards who have their names on two Stanley Cups.

Poile also deserves props for hiring Keith Allen as the Flyers' first coach.

In our first season, we won the West Division, which was composed of the league's six expansion teams. Poile and Allen put us on the right track.

Bud was also the first general manager of the Vancouver Canucks, and he was inducted into Hockey's Hall of Fame in 1990, a year after he received the Lester Patrick Trophy for outstanding service to hockey in the United States.

What I remember most about Bud is his passion for the game—and for winning. He had a temper and you could hear him screaming from the press box during the team's early years.

"We wanted to win so badly," Poile once told the *Inquirer*. "I wanted to be successful because I'd been in the minors so long —16 years I was there—and I wanted to be a big-league general manager. I just wanted to be the best, that's all. I was rather impatient, I guess."

Combined with his hockey smarts, that intensity, that drive to always seek to put a terrific team on the ice, is what made Bud such pillar in the front office.

Ed Snider and Joe Kadlec, who were both so important to me and my career with the Flyers.

CHAPTER 3
ALWAYS SEARCHING FOR THE NEXT BERNIE

Wh	hat are the odds that, 50 years after the Flyers started, the best goalie in franchise history would still be the one they selected first, in the NHL expansion draft for goaltenders in 1967?

But that is the case with the Flyers and Bernard Marcel Parent.

It seems like we've been trying to find another Bernie ever since.

Goalies are different. They have their own routines, their own little quirks. Take Bernie, for instance. He had to eat a sirloin streak with exactly 10 mushrooms before a game. And after his pregame nap, his routine included watching the Three Stooges because it put him in a good frame of mind.

Hey, whatever works.

Or, as former Flyer Bob Kelly once grinningly told *Philadelphia Magazine* when describing Bernie: "He's a Frenchman and a goaltender, so you know he's wacky."

Over the years, I have found some Flyers goalies to be loners—Michael Leighton fit in that category—and some to be very outgoing. Goalies grow up having frozen, vulcanized rubber pucks shot at them. And that's got to be difficult to start with. I think you have to have a different mentality to withstand the pressure that comes with that job. Goalies have to have a certain *savoir faire* about them.

During our 50-year history, we've had our share of goalies who were characters, but most of them were very good guys. Friendly guys. Regular guys who you liked spending time with. I guess Ilya Bryzgalov would be an exception, but all in all, the goalies we've had here were good people. Not many of them, however, could take over a game and give you the feeling they were difference-makers.

And then there was Bernie. Great guy, and he was in a class by himself in the net. But, remember, he was very raw when we selected him in the two-round goaltender section of the draft in '67. Los Angeles had the first pick and chose Terry Sawchuk, who had helped

Toronto win the Stanley Cup the previous season. We had the second pick and selected Bernie from the Boston Bruins. Bernie had divided the 1966–67 season with minor league Oklahoma City, where he had a 2.71 goals-against average, and Boston. In 18 games with last-place Bruins, he was 4–12–2 with an .890 save percentage and a 3.64 goals-against average.

In other words, no one was predicting he would turn into a Hall of Famer.

But he had great reflexes and all kinds of potential. He had so much potential, in fact, that according to Jay Greenberg's reporting in *Full Spectrum*, three teams approached the Flyers because they wanted to acquire him as the expansion draft continued.

The Flyers said no thanks.

Of course, early in 1971, we *did* trade Bernie to Toronto. Two years after that, we wisely got him back.

In our first year, we had two goalies who kept the guys loose. Bernie was always making jokes and was a bit of a clown, but Favy—Doug Favell, who we took with our second pick in the goalie expansion, also from the Bruins organization—was even more of a clown. He always liked to have fun. Always enjoyed himself. The two of them had played together in Oklahoma City, so they had a real good rapport. It's funny; as far as a practice goalie, Favy was not very good. He was better in games than in practice. Some games he was spectacular, other games he was just steady.

Bernie, on the other hand, was so consistent, and the bigger the game, the better he played. You look back at the old videos—with the equipment so much smaller than it is now—and it makes you appreciate him even more. He was and will remain the best that I've ever seen.

I've seen a lot of great goalies through the years, and it's hard to compare the different eras because of the change in equipment. But Marty Brodeur was certainly a big-game goalie. Ken Dryden and Terry Sawchuk stood out for me, as did Ed Belfour. As for the guys now, everybody is good; it's just that some stand out more in the big games. But it's hard to imagine a goalie who would be better than Bernie.

I remember our training camp through the Maritime provinces—New Brunswick, Nova Scotia, and Prince Edward Island—and staying in a hotel with a big fireplace, and Bernie making moose calls out front of the place, which was surrounded by woods in Halifax, Nova Scotia. The calls weren't for Moose Dupont. They were for *real* moose. "A-rooooooooooo! A-rooooooooooo," he's yelling. None ever came, but that was just Bernie being Bernie and keeping everybody loose.

This was during our early days, and we played four or five games in different cities in the Maritimes. We played mostly in tiny arenas that were homes for the junior teams. They were intrasquad games, and whichever team won would get to travel first to the next stop. So they would be in the next city before their teammates and would have a chance to explore the area, grab a beer, or just have some free time for themselves. The plane would drop them off, then come back and pick up the guys who lost the game.

It was great for me. I didn't have to announce anything. I just kept the stats, and I got to travel to some interesting places. Every day, we saw something new. We went to Charlottetown on Prince Edward Island and Allan Stanley, one of our veteran defensemen and a real classy guy, was like a God there. He had played on some great Toronto Maple Leafs teams and he was adored up there. But it was a good bonding experience for the players and it was good for the fans as well.

Goalie Carousel

Bernie suffered an unfortunate injury in 1979, and for most of the years since then, we've had a lot of different goalies here. Some didn't last long because of health reasons—Bruce Gamble, for instance, had a heart attack during a game, and that ended his career. And some lasted a few years and then moved on to another team.

Bobby "the Chief" Taylor was here longer than a lot of our goalies, but he didn't get into many games because he had the misfortune of backing up Bernie, who thrived on a lot of work and rarely went into a slump. Chief always kept everybody loose, and he was no shrinking violet. He was involved in some of our many altercations. He was in that big one against Vancouver where everybody went into the stands. He was such a great guy—easygoing off the ice—and after he retired, he was part of our broadcast team for our games on PRISM, and then spent a lot of years doing games in Tampa.

Wayne Stephenson was also Bernie's backup for a while until Bernie—who was just 33 and still playing very well—was accidentally hit in the eye by Jimmy Watson's stick in a 1979 game and never played again. Wayne had also played a lot when Bernie was injured in 1975–76 and we went back to the Finals for the third straight year but lost to Montreal. If you ran into Wayne in the street, you would have thought he was a CPA. He had that look, and that's exactly what he did after hockey. He was really good for us during a stretch. He was somebody who could come in off the bench cold and be very good. Some guys can do that; some other guys need to play a lot of games before they find their rhythm. Wayne could come in and give us a lift. Same with Bobby Froese, who played for us a little later.

Other than 1975–76, Wayne was our primary goalie for just one year (1978–79), and then Pete Peeters had a three-year run. Pete and Phil Myre shared the duties in 1979–80, and that season is best remembered for a tough loss to the Islanders in the Stanley Cup Finals, and, of course, our amazing 35-game unbeaten streak. Before that, the longest unbeaten streak in North American pro sports was 33 games by the NBA's Los Angeles Lakers in 1971–72. And we crushed the old NHL record of 28 straight unbeaten games, set by Montreal in 1977–78.

Some compared our amazing run to Joe DiMaggio's 56-game hitting streak in baseball, saying it would never be broken.

I would agree.

A Streak No One Saw Coming

Our streak kind of came out of nowhere. The previous season, we were brushed aside by Fred Shero's New York Rangers in five games in the Stanley Cup quarterfinals. We lost those four games by a combined score of 26–5, so it was not a happy summer.

Playing with a group of rookies and veterans who were still getting accustomed to one another, we opened the 1979–80 season with a 5–2 win over the New York Islanders at the Spectrum. But then memories of our playoff collapse resurfaced two nights later when we lost to the Atlanta Flames 9–2 at the Omni.

After that October 13 game, coach Pat Quinn said that the manner in which the Flyers responded to that embarrassing defeat "should tell us what kind of team we have."

We didn't lose again for 86 days.

It seemed like we got whatever we needed during the streak. If the goalies were off and we needed a lot of offense, we got it. If the offense was struggling or the opposing goalie was standing on his head, our goalie was even better. We got timely scoring, timely saves. And we had a hard-nosed team that took losing personally. I remember Quinn saying it was a once-in-a lifetime opportunity and that something like this might not come along again for 100 years. Well, I guess that would be in 2080.

When you look back on it, Peeters had 18 decisions (14–0–4) and Myre had 17 (11–0–6) during the streak. It's pretty incredible that Pete didn't lose a game that season until February. February! He was 22–0–5 until that loss.

Pete was a rookie during the Streak Season, but he had lost two games in a brief NHL stint with the Flyers the previous year.

Peeters and Myre withstood all the pressure that comes with a long streak. As the streak got longer, the media attention increased, and it became a major national story. Can you imagine what the pressure had to be like for the goalies? But what helped them is that they were both pretty easygoing guys and nothing seemed to bother them. And with each game, I think their confidence grew.

The skaters had lots of confidence, too. Rick MacLeish and Reggie Leach scored a lot of critical goals—they combined for 12 game-winning or game-tying scores during the 35-game run—but just about everybody chipped in and played an important role. I know it's a cliché, but it really was a total team effort. Even if we were down by a goal or two late in the game, you never felt like they were out of it, you always felt like they would find a way.

Bill Barber was clutch during the streak, scoring five game-winning goals, two that tied the score, and two shorthanded tallies.

Bobby Clarke had at least one point in 26 of the 35 games, and rookie sensation Brian Propp (points in 25 games during the streak), and MacLeish (points in 24 games) were also very consistent. During one stretch, Propp had points in nine straight games.

When we were on a roll in the 1970s, I made sure I did the same thing every night before a game. I'd be on the ice, right in front of the bench, as the players were coming off after their pregame skate. I'd watch them come off and Gary Dornhoefer would tap me on the butt with his stick as he left the ice and headed to the locker room. Every night. It was just a thing we did. It was like it created good vibes.

During our 35-game unbeaten streak, however, I didn't have any good-luck rituals, didn't wear the same time tie at every home game or do anything superstitious.

The streak finally ended in Minnesota, where we got spanked by the North Stars 7–1.

It was fun while it lasted. We packed arenas from coast to coast—four of our road opponents set new attendance records against us during the streak—and we received national coverage from all the networks, newspapers from around the globe, *Time*, and *Newsweek*.

If this had happened during today's 24-hour Information Age, we probably would have set a record for Twitter mentions.

During our streak, something embarrassing happened to me—and, I didn't know it at the time, but all 17,007 fans at the Spectrum knew it before me.

We were on our way to a blowout victory and the game was boring, so my eyes started scanning the crowd, and I said to the guy next to me, "Boy, there's a really good-looking blonde with a great tan in the first row." The next thing I know, the phone rings in my box. It's Joe Kadlec from up in the press box, and he says: "Lou, is she sitting on the right or the left?" It turns out I had left my microphone on, so the entire Spectrum heard me.

My wife, Ellen, laughs when someone brings that up...thank goodness. She's a good sport.

The Pelle Tragedy

Pelle Lindbergh was one of those guys to whom people gravitated. He was always upbeat, and he always had a smile.

He would have been considered a small goalie by today's standards, but he had tremendous ability, tremendous reflexes, and a tremendous desire. Bernie was his goalie coach and a lot of people thought Pelle was going to be *the* goalie here for a long, long time—then a tragic car accident took his life in 1985. He seemed on track to become one of the NHL's elite goalies for the next decade or so. All goalies have an ability to anticipate plays, but Pelle seemed to be a step above them all. He saw the game in front of him so well. People talk about how Wayne Gretzky saw the game better than anyone. He said he would always go to where the puck was going to be. Pelle had that, too. He saw the game better than most. He had great anticipation and would be able to predict where a play was going.

Fair or not, a lot of folks labeled Pelle as the next Bernie during his time here. That seemed fitting, because Bernie had been his idol when Pelle was playing in Sweden. And Bernie had him on track to be one of the best we've ever had. He was special and everybody knew it. Besides all his talents, Pelle had a burning desire to succeed. Like Ron Hextall, who played goalie a few years later for the Flyers, Pelle was the ultimate competitor and someone who had a deep passion for hockey.

They say that goalies are "on the edge," and, in a way, that applied to Pelle off the ice. And I think that cost him. I will always remember the shock and the sadness at his service at Old Swedes Church on Washington Avenue and Columbus. And I'll never forget how eloquent Dave Poulin was. Dave was our captain and he delivered the eulogy; it was a beautiful tribute to someone who left us way too soon.

It was just a sad time for everybody, and Bobby Froese was thrown into a difficult situation. He replaced Pelle after his death, and no one would want to become the No. 1 goalie after a situation like that. Bob was a happy-go-lucky guy, a good goalie, and he's a minister now. He came in and saved our bacon, that's for sure.

After Froese, Ron Hextall came in and it didn't take long before he became a fan favorite. You see Hexy now, and he is very deliberate and calculating as a general manager, but he wasn't as patient on the ice. Far from it! He was probably the most passionate goalie we've ever had here. He did not want to be messed with by opposing players. He did not like it when players crowded him. He loved to use his stick to keep people away, and he was very fiery, very emotional. He didn't like it when he lost. Now I know you can probably say that about all goalies, but Hexy took it to another level.

Now, he's very measured as a GM, but he was the opposite as a player. I can remember a game at Chicago Stadium during Hexy's rookie season (1986–87). We're winning 5–4, late in the game, and Chicago was a tough place for us to win. Hexy had given up four goals, but it could have been eight if he hadn't been playing so well. The Blackhawks are throwing everything at the net, and Hexy is holding them off, making a ton of great saves. Up in the press box, we were told he was going to be named the game's second star, so Joe Kadlec, our public relations director, and I went downstairs and leaned against the glass—and, just like that, Chicago scored with about a minute left. That tied the game. They didn't change the stars, so Hexy was still going to be No. 2 and skate on the ice and take a bow after the game was over. Joe said to me, "Tell Hexy he's the No. 2 star and I'll go into the locker room for interviews."

I took one look at Hexy as he came off the ice slamming his stick and I said to myself, "No way am I telling him anything!" There was no way I was going to stop him and say, "Excuse me, Ron. You've been named the No. 2 star. Can you hold up?" He marched right past me, stick swinging, and went straight to the locker room to cool off. So they announced the second star and no one came out. It was my fault, but there were extenuating circumstances.

People remember Hexy for being an antagonist because of the way he would use his stick to chop at opposing players, and for going after Montreal's Chris Chelios in 1989—he was retaliating for Chelios elbowing Brian Propp to the head earlier in that playoff series. But he was a terrific goalie, and he was such an innovator. He was so good at firing passes out to teammates to start a rush down the other end. He played in 66 games in his first year and led us to the Stanley Cup Finals, where we lost to Gretzky and a powerhouse Edmonton Oilers team in seven hard-fought games. Hexy was so dominating in the playoffs that he became just the fourth player from a losing team to win the Conn Smythe Trophy.

When Hexy was inducted into the Flyers Hall of Fame in 2008, I had a brainstorm. I had one of his sticks at home, and he used to ring them off the post all the time. Back and forth, back and forth before each period started. I guess it was his superstition. So when we inducted him, I brought the stick in and I had the ice guys bring the goal out. He was on the red carpet for the ceremony and I was introducing him and I said, "Hexy, step over to the goal and ring those posts one more time." I took the mic over by the goal cage and all you heard was *bing-bing-bing* as he banged his stick against them one last time. He was laughing, and the crowd loved it. I told him about it beforehand and he was fine with it, like when Schultzy (Dave Schultz) went to the penalty box one last time when he was inducted into our Hall of Fame.

When Hexy first played here, it looked like he had a chance to be the next Bernie, but he had some injury problems that slowed him down and ended up getting traded to Quebec as part of the famous 1992 Eric Lindros deal, and then came back here in a 1994 trade with the New York Islanders. He never became Bernie, but he was a very good goalie and, of course, everybody remembers him becoming the first goalie to shoot a puck into the net and score a goal.

Hexy was a workhorse in his first three seasons with us, playing more than 60 games each season. He was injured for most of his fourth year, and Ken Wregget took over. Ken was kind of a journeyman, but a great guy and he was here for a few years. After Hexy was traded, Dominic Roussel and Tommy Soderstom were our main goalies for a couple years before Hexy came back and almost led us to the Cup in '97.

Tommy was small and quick, and he was a good person. He had had a heart procedure earlier in his career, and I remember telling him that one of my friends, Jason Raff, was going to have the same procedure. I told him he was scared to death to have it. Tommy told me to bring him in so he could talk to him. So I brought Jason in and they talked for a half hour and it calmed him down. Tommy said, "Make sure you let me know how it works out." Jason had the procedure, and he did fine.

After that, Hexy left the second time, and we continued to search for the right guy. Was it going to be an oldie but goodie, the Beezer, John Vanbiesbrouck? Garth Snow? Sean Burke?

Beezer had so much class. A mild-mannered guy who always had time for you, he nearly won a Stanley Cup in Florida in 1996, and he was solid for us in his two years here in 1998–99 and 1999–2000.

Herman Munster in the Nets?

Here's a quick story about Garth Snow, or "Snowy," as we called him: He went to watch a lacrosse game, and he paid close to attention to the goalie, whose shoulder pads he liked. Garth had a brainstorm. He borrowed a set of the lacrosse shoulder pads, and it looked like he was wearing four-foot-by-four-foot pads. Remember the padded shoulders that Herman Munster wore? That was Snowy. They were unbelievably big. It only lasted for a couple games. I guess they said it wasn't the proper equipment and banned it. Hey, whatever you can do to get an edge, right? Do it until they say no.

It's funny that Garth became the general manager of the Islanders and Hexy became our GM. I had no inclination that was going to happen back in the day. I was surprised when Snowy got the job with the Islanders. Some people, I guess, are more analytical, but I didn't know that side of either of them back when they played.

By 2000, we had a goalie who had played for a number of years in the Czech League, Roman Cechmanek, who was a good goaltender but was also good at throwing his teammates under the bus.

Cecho played pretty well, but if he was talking to the media about a goal he allowed, he would blame his teammates for things that happened to him. That didn't make him very popular in the room. And he did some strange things. He was the first guy I ever saw who would use his head to make a save. A shot would be over the goal and he would head it to the side. Never saw anything like it. It was like one of those things where you ask yourself, "Did I just see what I thought

47

I saw?" And you'd look at the replay and it was like, "I'll be damned. He *did* make a save with a head-butt." The first time I saw him do it was in a road game and I got to see the replay of it a few times.

I don't know if he was a soccer player or not, but maybe that's where the header came in. A lot of our guys in recent years kick around a soccer ball in the hallway to get ready for a game. It's a way to loosen up, and I think it began when more Europeans came over and started playing in the NHL. Now it seems like most of the players do that before a game, whether they're European or not.

Maybe Cecho used to play forward on a soccer team when he was growing up and he got used to heading a ball. I don't know for sure, but I know it was strange-looking thing to see on a hockey rink.

Brian Boucher followed Cecho, and I can't say enough about Boosh. He was always a class act, always accessible. And his personality is showing through now with the TV work he's doing with the networks.

Boosh didn't become another Bernie, but he was a good goalie in his own right. He was the goalie in two of our most memorable wins in franchise history. He beat the Penguins 2–1 in that epic five-overtime playoff game in 2000, and no Flyers fan will ever forget him outplaying the great Henrik Lundqvist in a shootout as we beat the Rangers on the final day of the regular season in 2010 to sneak into the playoffs. If we had lost that game, we went home. No win, no playoffs. And then we got hot at just the right time and beat the Devils in the first round before coming back from a three-games-to-none series deficit and shocking Boston. Next, we ousted Montreal as Michael Leighton was almost unbeatable, collecting three shutouts to put us into the Stanley Cup Finals.

We lost, of course, to Chicago in the Finals, but if we had won the Cup that year, the magnitude of Boosh's win over King Henrik and the Rangers would have grown and grown. As it was, it's still a very special part of our history, but some of the luster was taken off because we didn't quite finish our remarkable playoff run and fell two wins shy of the Stanley Cup.

I'll never forget the emotion on the ice when Boosh stopped Olli Jokinen to give us the shootout win and put us into the playoffs. The bench emptied, and I never saw Boosh dance like he did after his game-clinching save. Danny Briere was the first to jump into his arms, followed by Claude Giroux, who had scored the shootout winner, and then Boosh was engulfed in a sea of orange jerseys.

As my friend Bernie Parent would say, it was a beautiful thing.

Boosh wasn't the kind of guy who would celebrate that way, but he was caught up in the moment—the whole city was—and you could really feel the fans getting behind us from that point through each round of the playoffs. We almost seemed like a team of destiny, especially after we came back from that 3–0 hole against the Bruins.

When a game ends like it did in that 2010 regular-season finale against the Rangers, I go right to work. I have announcements to make and paperwork to take care of. But after Boosh made that save, I know I cheered—with the mic off. And I don't cheer too often. I was like, "Yessssssssssssssss!." It was chaos, but the kind of chaos you like. And it was a culmination of a long, hard struggle to get into the Stanley Cup playoffs.

"Hopefully we can do something with our lifeline here and use the excitement and euphoria from this win—and from our last little stretch of games here—to propel us and do good things in the playoffs," defenseman Chris Pronger said after the emotional victory.

After that game, I'm in the locker room and Boosh stops me. He always used to kid me and ask why the players get a case of Tastykakes when they score goals but the goalies never got anything. He said to me that day, "So *now* do I get a case of Tastykakes?"

Looking back, I should have run to Wawa and bought all the butterscotch Krimpets that were left in the store. He deserved them.

In the years just before our 2010 run, we had Robert Esche, Antero Niittymaki—or Nitty, as everybody called him—and Marty Biron in goal. Again, we were always searching for a guy who would be a long-term solution, but it seemed like no one lasted for more than a few years. We were always wondering where the next Bernie was coming from. We had a lot of revolving goalies and, for the most part, the team was so-so.

Bob Esche was a wonderful guy who never let things bother him; he was steady but not spectacular and he then finished his career playing in Russia and is now president of the Utica Comets, the AHL affiliate of the Vancouver Canucks.

Nitty had a great 2006 Olympics with Finland—they won the silver medal and he was named the MVP of the entire tournament—and everybody was excited that he was going to have a long career here, but he had a lot of hip problems and that greatly affected his career. He was serviceable, but didn't set the world on fire. Sometimes, it was almost like: who's next?

Marty Biron was a good goalie for us. Good but not great, but he was one of the all-time good guys. And the women loved him. You'd see a picture of him with his blue eyes piercing through the mask. I don't know how many women have asked me, "Are his eyes really that blue?" He had a magnanimous personality, and he was friends with everybody. Some guys remember who you are and just have a great human spirit about them. Marty was one of those guys.

Some guys are with the organization for a short time and don't take the time to get to know you. Marty took the time to get to know everybody. That's what's good about this team right now. They're great guys and all take the time to get to know everybody. They interact and they generally like being here. Sometimes, I think players feel like they're ships passing through the night. They feel this is just a stop for them in what they hope will be a long career. With the team we have here now, I get the feeling they're not treating this is a stop along the way. They're here for the long haul. This is their home. They're a very down-to-earth group of guys, and I have good feelings about this team. They're good people.

Kane's Bizarre Goal

In 2010, a year in which we came so close to not making the playoffs at all and then so close to winning the Stanley Cup, we had a lot of injuries with our goalies, and three of them played almost an equal amount of games—Boosh, Leighton, and Ray Emery.

Michael carried us in the Eastern Conference finals with the three shutouts against Montreal, and the whole team played great defense in front of him. But unfortunately, when you bring up Michael Leighton's name, the first thing everybody thinks of is Patrick Kane's bizarre overtime goal that gave Chicago the Cup in Game 6 at the Wells Fargo Center. It seemed like Kane was the only one who knew the shot went into the net. It was a bizarre play, because everybody froze for a few seconds after he shot it. Everybody except Kane. He went around the net, came out the other side, and started celebrating by skating joyously down the other end. The light never went on to signify a goal, but Kane knew.

Kane took the shot from the left wing, which was my side of the ice. You can only see so much from where I sit, and, to be honest, I couldn't tell for sure if it went in. But from the way Patrick reacted—throwing his gloves, throwing his stick in the air—I said to myself, "The puck went in." I remember announcing that the play was under review, but I knew it was going to stand. The refs didn't see it and Augie Conte, the head of off-ice officials, said they were going to look at a replay, which of course, confirmed the goal.

Leighton was hurt the next year and Sergei Bobrovsky, a promising rookie, beat out Boosh for the starting job. I loved Bob. Nice guy, very friendly. I learned how to say "How you doing?" in Russian—*privyet*—from him. But we had revolving goalies in the playoffs that year, and, after it ended, Ed Snider said he never wanted to go through that again. In hindsight, we didn't realize what we had in Bob. He was a young kid whose game was still growing. But we went out and signed the best goalie out there on the free-agent market, Ilya Bryzgalov. Bryz was more than different. I tell my wife, he may be the only guy I didn't like in my 50 years with the team. And he gave me a couple reasons for it.

I would see him before every game in the runway, looking right at me. And yet when I interviewed him at the Flyers Wives Carnivals, he would say, "I don't know you from the runway." He embarrassed me more than once. Another time I was interviewing him for the Carnival and he said, "I want a box with my name on it filled with money and I want to be shot into space." That was Bryz. He was a space cadet. He would say strange things all the time, and I got the feeling there was uneasiness in the locker room when he was around. Some guys liked him, some didn't, but he was a distraction.

We ended up buying out Bryz's big contract because we got Steve Mason in a trade with Columbus, and he had some really good years. Steve had a challenge in his personal life in the 2015–16 season and kind of lost focus for a little bit. Understandably so, because he went through a tough situation. But he regrouped and finished the year strongly. To me, he and Michal Neuvirth can both be No. 1 goalies. For a lot of years, we were searching for a true No. 1, but in 2016–17 we had two goalies who, when playing up to their capabilities, could be the starter on most NHL teams. That's a luxury we hadn't had in a long time.

Both goalies, however, struggled for a good part of the 2016–17 season. Maybe the weight of their contract situation played a part in it. No one really knows. Both knew they could become unrestricted free agents in the summer, so, in effect, they were playing for contract renewals.

Bottom line: we are still searching for our next Bernie.

Maybe it will be one of the three Flyers prospects who competed in the World Junior Championships that ended on January 5, 2017: Canada's Carter Hart, Sweden's Felix Sandstrom, or Slovakia's Matej Tomek.

Or maybe Anthony Stolarz or Alex Lyon, two goalies in our system, will emerge.

All five young goaltenders have outstanding potential and it will be interesting to watch their development in upcoming seasons.

CHAPTER 4

LEADERS OF THE PACK

There are a lot of things that make a good leader. Yes, it helps if the leader is a great player, but it's not a prerequisite.

Joe Watson, for instance, was a good player, but he wasn't a perennial all-star. Yet, to me, Joe was a great leader because of the way he could rally the troops and they way he had universal respect in the locker room.

Bob Clarke was, without question, the best leader in franchise history. He was a rarity—a world-class player who always worked harder than anyone else on the ice. Always. That is the most important ingredient in a leader. Just being a great player doesn't necessarily mean you will have great leadership qualities. But Clarkie was the complete package, someone who was wildly talented and someone who refused to be outworked.

Fred Shero used to say that the best players are the ones who stay focused on *their* tasks. One of his sayings: Save time thinking you can do the other fellow's job better than he can—and put that energy into doing your job better.

The leaders are the ones who get their teammates to keep that focus, keep that direction.

We have had a slew of great leaders in our 50-year history, some of whom were captains, and some of whom weren't. With apologies to the many inspirational players who are not on my list, here is my Sweet 16 of the best leaders in Flyers history, ranked in order:

1. Bob Clarke
2. Dave Poulin
3. Keith Primeau
4. Eric Lindros
5. Chris Pronger
6. Rod Brind'Amour
7. Claude Giroux

8. Ed Van Impe
9. Mel Bridgman
10. Rick Tocchet
11. Mark Howe
12. Eric Desjardins
13. Kimmo Timonen
14. Bill Barber
15. Bernie Parent
16. Joe Watson

As I mentioned, many others could have made this list, but these are the guys who stood out to me.

No. 1 has to be Clarkie. He played hard in practice and played hard in games. When there was something that needed to happen on the ice, he made it happen. When there was something that needed to be addressed, he addressed it. He was not afraid to stand up and give everybody grief if he didn't think they were playing up to speed. And he had a quick wit. I heard that in the penalty box, where he would yap with the referee. He never thought he deserved a penalty. Never. Ever. I remember him telling referee Andy Van Hellemond, "Andy, remember when you went back to the Western League because you were terrible? You're up here now, and you're *still* terrible."

Clarkie epitomized leadership.

Dave Poulin was another great leader and, like Clarkie, he didn't let injuries bother him. He played hurt. Dave scored a lot of important goals for us, and the thing I remember the most is that he was always well-spoken. He always handled himself very professionally, and it's no surprise that he's doing TV work now. You can never go wrong hiring a Dave Poulin—whether it's as a coach, in the front office, or in the media. He even did a great job filling in on our radio broadcast one night for Steve Coates when Coatesy was out because of Achilles' surgery in 2017.

Whatever he's been asked to do, Dave does a great job. If you need something done, he's the kind of guy you go to.

When Pelle Lindbergh died, Dave spoke at the service, and he could not have been more eloquent. He talked about Pelle and how he touched everybody, and how we were better people for having known him. He had everybody's eyes filling up with tears. Dave just always had his act together, on and off the ice.

I have Keith Primeau third on my list, and I didn't realize what a great leader he was until I saw him play on a day-in, day-out basis. He was a guy who stepped up in the room, and on the ice he could intimidate players from other teams with his size. He had the size and was not afraid to drop the gloves when he had to, as Eric Lindros did during his early years.

Keith scored a lot of big goals for us, and I think when you mention his name, the first thing Flyers fans probably think of is the goal he scored to beat the Penguins in Pittsburgh in 2000. That ended a five-overtime classic that was the third-longest game in NHL history—and the longest since 1936. (Even I wasn't born yet!)

Like Poulin, Eric Lindros was a captain here for six years. Only Bob Clarke (nine years) served as our captain for more seasons. Younger fans may not know that Eric was drafted by the Quebec Nordiques but refused to go there. The Nordiques then traded him. The problem was, two teams—the Flyers and New York Rangers—thought they had acquired him and it was up to an arbitrator to decide. I was in Maryland for business at the time, and a friend of mine put his phone up to the radio when the announcement was made. That's how I found out they had ruled in the Flyers' favor and he would come here.

Before the 1992–93 season, we paid a heavy price to get him—six players, two draft picks, and $15 million to the Nordiques—but he helped turn the franchise around. The guy was a bull. There was no stopping him. No one in the league had his combined size (6'4", 240 pounds) and talent at that time.

We needed somebody like him, because we were a few years away from leaving the Spectrum and opening our new building, which was then known as the CoreStates Center. We needed some excitement on this team, and he provided it. And then when we put Mikael Renberg and John LeClair with him, well, it sealed the deal. No teams could stop that line. They were just awesome together.

And the thing about Eric was he would always try passes that nobody tries nowadays—the flip from behind the net over sticks. He always felt comfortable throwing it out front because John was always there, waiting to do damage. If Eric threw it out front, there was a good chance John would find a way to put the puck on his stick. They had an amazing chemistry.

Eric's parents were always around, and they got involved in a lot of things. Eric was overmanaged, I guess. And I think Clarkie, who was then our GM, took the stance that once somebody becomes an NHL player, they should make their own decisions. There were times that Eric's parents wanted to know why he was playing with certain players; they wanted him to be able to utilize his talents to the fullest. It was interference that was unprecedented anywhere in this league.

But on the ice, Eric was the most dominant player in almost every game, night in and night out. He was exciting, and he sold tickets and got people into the building. We've never had a player like him, with his size and skill. That said, I think Clarkie was the best player we have ever had, because he did it night in and night out over a long period of time. Eric didn't take nights off, but he was injured a lot, and he just wasn't here that long. We never won a Stanley Cup with him.

Eric always played hard, always gave it 100 percent. He took on all challengers, and that's what made him a great leader. When Eric came into the league, people were calling him the next Gretzky. It's tough to live up to those expectations, but he tried his damndest.

Years earlier, Mel Bridgman didn't arrive with the same fanfare as Eric, even though he was—and still is—the only player in our history who was drafted No. 1 overall.

Bridgman was taken No. 1 in 1975, and he was one of the most underrated captains in our history. He was probably one of the 10 toughest guys to ever play here, and he was also a very solid player.

The guys who are drafted No. 1 nowadays seem to be players who have great offensive talents. Mel was a complete player. Played the game hard both ways and wasn't afraid to speak up in the locker room and always led by example. And he was one of the guys who always stepped up for his teammates on the ice. He was just a prototypical, hardnosed player who was deeply respected in the locker room.

Roddy Brind'Amour was like Bridgman in that he was the ultimate team guy. He did everything. Played in all situations and he was a warrior. Always. He never stopped. And he was a workout freak who pushed himself to be the best he could be. In other words, he was the definition of a leader.

Mark Howe and Claude Giroux are two other guys who were deeply respected—and I have them both on my list. Claude is like Mark in that he leads by example, though G seems to be getting more assertive and more outspoken with his teammates as he has matured. G plays the game so hard and that's how he leads. He never takes a shift off, and that rubs off on his teammates. And I've seen him play through a lot of pain in recent years, but he refuses to sit out.

I think having Chris Pronger here for a couple years helped G— and a lot of guys. To be able to talk with somebody who had that experience and that presence—and see how he controls the room— I think has helped him learn how to handle certain situations that come up.

As for Mark Howe, he was a quiet guy who was the best defenseman we've ever had. We called him Howie, and some think he was the best player not to ever win the Norris Trophy, which is given to the league's top defenseman. I agree with that. He could do everything—play up, play back—and be a big difference-maker. He and Brad McCrimmon were a tandem that was terrific. Mark came from hockey royalty, but he never big-timed anybody. He was always modest, always classy. Every time I'd see his dad, Gordie, he'd playfully strangle me from behind and then give me his elbows. Great man.

In his own quiet way, Mark had such a presence about him that made the players look up to him. Everybody has their own way of leading, and Mark's way was simple: go about your business, make big plays, and always put the team above personal achievements.

Eric Desjardins wasn't overly outspoken, either, but he led in every other way. He was a great leader and a great player. He made everyone around him better. One of the many things he did well was his uncanny ability to keep the puck in at the blue line. He found ways.

Eric was such a steady player for so long here, and no matter who he played with, he made them better. He played with Bundy (Chris Therien) for a long time, and he made him a better player, no question.

Usually, when a guy is named captain it's cause for a celebration. But that wasn't the case with Desjardins, who was thrown into a tough situation. Lindros had the "C" stripped after he criticized the training staff, and Clarkie made Desjardins the captain.

With Mr. Hockey, Gordie Howe, in the 1980s.

Ron Hextall made my original leader list, but he ended up on the cutting-room floor. That, however, doesn't diminish his leadership qualities. Hexy wasn't a captain, but he was someone who hated to lose maybe as much as anybody I've ever seen, and to me, that translated into leadership. He was all fire. The players saw that and followed suit. They developed that same kind of attitude.

You knew that if Hexy lost a game, he needed to cool off and it probably was not a good idea to talk to him right away. He took losing personally.

He was fearless in the net and around it. And opposing players stayed away from him because of his stick. Billy Smith was the same way with the Islanders. Hexy thought the area in front of the net was his, and if you entered it, you were trespassing. That was his territory. I can remember him chopping down guys with a whack to the leg.

And everybody remembers him going after Chris Chelios. That was Hexy. He defended our guys all the time.

I guess when you think of leaders, you don't think of goalies too often, but Hexy certainly fit the bill. So did Bernie Parent, because of the way he performed and the way he picked everybody up, time and time again. He kept everybody loose in the locker room, and that made for a very relaxed atmosphere. He just had such a likable personality. and he helped create a great bond in that locker room.

Pronger was great in the room. When you talk about someone who commanded respect, that's Pronger. It's just a shame he had the concussion problems and wasn't here too long. He was a great leader his whole career, not just here. I don't think it's any coincidence that a lot of teams went to the Finals when he was with then. I just wish he had been here longer. I think we were destined to have some great teams with him, but when Chris went down, the whole defense changed. We've been looking for a true No. 1 defenseman ever since. In 2016–17, Ivan Provorov was our top defenseman in his rookie year, and he looks like he is going to be a great player, but it will take some time before he commands the respect that Chris earned.

Kimmo Timonen was never a captain here, but not because he wasn't worthy. Kimmo was a great leader and tremendous player. He was an alternate captain and the players listened to him because he didn't pull punches. He was the same way with the media. Every time he was interviewed after a game, he didn't sugarcoat things. He spoke the truth and wasn't afraid to stir things up and criticize if he felt it needed to be said.

Rick Tocchet also gets high marks for leadership. Not only was he a great scorer, but he would drop his gloves and pick up for somebody if it was needed. He was a good player with great hands and he continued his leadership in the coaching world.

Bill Barber is another guy who was a terrific leader who took that into the coaching ranks. It may sound funny to say a guy who made the Hockey Hall of Fame is underrated, but I think that was the case with Billy. Because he played on the same teams and same line as Clarkie, he was overshadowed.

To me, leaders are guys who are not afraid to stand up in front of their teammates and call people out, if necessary. There's a risk of alienating yourself from some teammates, but the good leaders don't worry about that. They speak from the heart and speak honestly for the good of the team.

The Hall Calls

Interestingly, six of the players I consider to be the best leaders in Flyers history are also in Hockey's Hall of Fame: Parent, Clarke, Barber, Howe, Pronger, and Lindros. And maybe one day Giroux will join them.

Lindros was the latest Hall of Famer, and it was great to see him inducted in 2016 because I know there were some hockey observers who didn't think he played long enough to be honored.

"There's a lot of luck that goes along with this," said the man who was a six-time all-star, the league's MVP in 1994–95, and a trailblazer of sorts for how concussions are handled in the NHL. "But there's a lot of support behind the scenes that you get, and it's nice to look back on and truly appreciate."

Eric's career spanned parts of 13 years, but, primarily because of concussions, he played 70 or more games in just four of those seasons.

But if you look at how dominating he was when he played, you can understand why he went into the Hall. He had amazing production: 865 points and 372 goals in 760 games.

To me, Eric definitely deserves to be in the Hall of Fame. His teams were in contention all the time, and his numbers are very strong. He averaged 1.36 points per game during the Flyers portion of his career, which is—by far—tops in franchise history. And if you look at his entire career, his points-per-game average (1.14) is 17ᵗʰ in NHL history. I know Eric has his detractors because of all the games he missed, but when you look at what he accomplished when he did play, it's difficult to make a case that he shouldn't be in the Hall.

When Eric first came into the league, he was a kick-ass player. You didn't fool with him, because if you did, he was going to clean you up. But he spent a lot of time in the penalty box. There were a lot of two- and five-minute penalties, a lot of five-minute penalties. But because he was fighting, it gave him a lot of room on the ice. The Flyers didn't want him in the box and may have asked him to stay away from the fighting because they wanted to see him *on* the ice.

To me, that was one of the key factors that changed the way opponents played him. When teams saw he was reluctant to retaliate, they ran at him really bad and took shots at him. In his early years, he had a lot of room on the ice because teams knew if you tangled with him, there was a good chance there was going to be a fight that followed. But either Eric himself or management thought he was spending too much time in the penalty box, so he wasn't as combative after the first couple years and, as a result, opponents hounded him more and gave him less room to operate. They weren't as worried about Eric dropping the gloves.

The good news was that with Eric on the ice more, he and his line thrived. The bad news: he absorbed more physical punishment, and that contributed to his concussions.

At the Hall of Fame ceremony in 2016, Eric spoke candidly.

"Looking back, I wish I wasn't quite as physical," admitted Lindros, who spent eight of his 13 seasons with the Flyers and retired from the NHL when he was 34. "I wish I had pulled it back about 25 percent and saved some of that…. A collision is a collision and it takes a toll on bodies."

Eric's line was breathtaking. There was a buzz from the crowd when they got on the ice and they just swarmed the opposing goalie. Ed Snider once was quoted as saying the Legion of Doom unit—Lindros centering LeClair and Renberg—was the best line he had ever seen. Those were strong words when you consider that the team's LCB line—Clarke centering Barber and Leach—had two Hall of Famers on it, along with a guy (Leach) who once scored an amazing 80 goals in a season, including 19 in the playoffs.

Lindros' line just overpowered people. Eric was 6'4", and weighed between 229 and 240 during his playing days, LeClair was 6'3", 226, and Renberg was 6'2", 218. They won most battles for loose pucks, and if they had possession, not many opponents were big enough to take it away from any of them.

During his Hall of Fame acceptance speech, Lindros thanked LeClair and Renberg, each of whom attended the ceremony, "for their intensity and joy. I was lucky to be your centerman."

In an emotional ending to his speech, Lindros called his brother, Brett, onto the stage. Brett's NHL career also ended because of concussions. "I would like to close this chapter of my life with you by my side," he said.

Classy guy, that Eric Lindros.

Besides Clarkie, Big E is the only Flyer to win the MVP award, capturing the Hart Trophy in 1995. Eric cared as much as almost anybody who ever wore the Orange and Black, and that was exemplified when he made a stirring acceptance speech after winning the Hart.

Eric was teary-eyed and his voice cracked with emotion toward the end of his MVP speech in 1995.

"In closing, I'd like to say thank you to the fans of Philadelphia who supported us even when we weren't so the good," he said.

He paused. He swallowed hard and spoke from the heart. "We're getting better and we're going to do it," he added as he voice broke up.

But we never won a Cup during Eric's eight seasons in Philadelphia. We did reach the Finals in 1997, but lost to Detroit in four straight games. The Red Wings did a great job on the Lindros line, so we are still searching for our first Cup since 1975.

"I'm shocked about what happened," Lindros said at the time. "It was just a blur. We couldn't stop the bleeding."

One week later, the bleeding continued. Terry Murray—who had called the Flyers' play in the finals a "choking situation"—was fired.

I liked Terry. He was a straightforward guy and spoke his mind. He was a defensive-minded coach, and maybe his coaching style had something to do with the firing, too—besides the fact you can't be calling your team out like that. Later, Terry said he should have chosen his words differently. It's one thing to say the team isn't playing up to its ability, but another to say it is choking. That was the ultimate insult, and I think Clarke, our GM at the time, thought it would be difficult for the players to ever respect Terry again after those comments. Part of me was surprised at the firing—Terry's teams played the game the right way—but the other part of me could understand it. He insulted the guys who took his team to the Stanley Cup Finals.

I kind of like when your team emphasizes defense—and tries to hold the opponent down and look for opportunities. That was Terry's style.

Hakstol's Impressive Debut

I see a little bit of Terry Murray in Dave Hakstol. Dave's teams play smart, positional hockey. They don't play the attacking style that marked Peter Laviolette's teams. They play two-way hockey and, like Murph's teams, seize the scoring opportunity when it arises. They don't try to force things.

Hakstol was named our coach before the 2015–16 season, coming straight from the college-coaching ranks at North Dakota, where his teams were powerhouses. Still, he was making a gigantic leap into the NHL, and a lot of folks were skeptical that he could make the jump. It's one thing to do it in college, where it's easier to get the players' attention. It's a lot more difficult in the NHL, where you are trying to motivate millionaires, trying to get every ounce of potential out of them.

But in his first year, Hak silenced the critics. Quickly. It only took a few months for the Flyers to grasp his system, and over the second half of the season, we were one of the NHL's most consistent teams. We accumulated 84 points the previous season, but in Hak's first year, we collected 96 points and earned a playoff berth before losing to powerful Washington in six hard-fought games. Dave got everything possible out of that team, and that's an indication of a high-quality coach.

I guess we shouldn't have been surprised. Hak's teams earned NCAA tournament berths during each of his 11 seasons at North Dakota. And his teams had more Frozen Four appearances (seven) in that span than any team in the country.

If you back up a couple of years, we went from an offensive-minded coach in Peter Laviolette to a much more defensive-minded coach in Craig Berube...and then to Hak. This team was going in two different directions under Lavy and Chief. Totally different styles. I think Hak added a lot of stability here. In Hak's first year, the team played the game the right way. They covered players, they were in the right place at the right time. Nothing fancy, but just good, solid fundamental hockey. I think having a former college coach come in was a good move at the time.

We finished 41–27–14 in Hak's first year, which was outstanding when you consider that some of the players didn't have great seasons and we struggled to score goals. For the most part, the finishers didn't finish, but we were still very competitive.

When Hak gets some of the top young prospects here, I think they will continue to improve under him and this team will make strides. That said, we need to get some finishers, some scorers. When the young prospects and the finishers get together, this team will take off.

People ask me if Hak reminds me of anyone, and one of the names thrown out there is Mike Keenan, who coached for the Flyers for four seasons (from 1984–85 to 1987–88.) I don't really see many similarities between the two, to be honest.

Mike was a great coach. He got a lot out of a lot of players for a long time. I don't see a lot of parallels between him and Hak, other than they both had college coaching experience, though Mike didn't go directly from the collegiate ranks to the NHL. I think Mike grated on the players after a while, but while he was here, the franchise grew and got better. And, remember; a little over a year after he got here, Keenan had to somehow get the players' minds back on hockey after Pelle Lindbergh's shocking death in 1985. It was a difficult situation, to say the least, and Mike got a lot of help from Poulin, one of the classiest captains to ever play for the Orange and Black.

Keenan was a young pup when he was hired—and promptly took us to the 1985 Stanley Cup Finals in his first season. He was just 35, and he had the reputation for being a disciplinarian from his days at St. Lawrence University and the University of Toronto. But unlike Hak, Mike had some pro coaching experience. He had been with the Buffalo Sabres' AHL affiliate in Rochester before the Flyers hired him, so he had a feel for the professional game. In fact, he led Rochester to the AHL title the year before he took the Flyers' job.

The biggest similarity between Hak and Keenan is the fresh approach the organization took in hiring them. Instead of going after a recycled coach like so many teams do, the Flyers went outside the box with both hires.

Another similarity: Keenan was the first coaching hire made by new general manager Bob Clarke, while Hakstol was Ron Hextall's first coaching hire as a GM. Craig Berube had already been in place when Hexy took over, and he lasted just a year under Ron.

When Hakstol was hired, Hexy said he had run a pro-style program at North Dakota. I think that and the fact he developed about 20 players that reached the NHL—including Jonathan Toews, T.J. Oshie, Travis Zajac, Matt Greene, and Drew Stafford—is why Hexy rolled the dice. That and the fact that Hexy wanted to put his stamp on the team and give it a new identity moving forward.

At the time, Hexy said he wasn't going to choose someone because he was the people's choice or the most popular choice, but that he wanted someone who was right for the franchise "today, next year, and moving forward. Dave was the right choice."

When he was named our coach, Dave was 47—12 years older than Keenan. Not that he was old, but he seems even a lot younger than his age. Maybe that comes from being around young college kids for so long. I'm not sure of the reason, but I know he has a youthfulness and energy about him that is contagious.

Keenan had that, too, but after four years, the players tuned him out and he was fired. At the time, I remember Clarkie saying the players had "lost their enthusiasm" to play for Mike. That seems to be a common occurrence in the NHL after four years. That seems to be the usual shelf life for coaches nowadays before they move on to another franchise.

Maybe things will be different with Hak.

CHAPTER 5

LEMIEUX'S RETURN: FLYERS FANS AT THEIR BEST

Most people are familiar with me because of my work with the Flyers for the last half century.

But I've done some work for many other Philly sports teams. Unfortunately, most of them are no longer around. I think I might lead the area in working for teams that have left town. I hope I'm not the one who chased them out.

Let's see now...I've done some work for the Bell of the World Football League, the Fever of the Major Indoor Soccer League, the Atoms of the North American Soccer League, and the original Wings of the National Lacrosse League.

But I didn't chase all the teams out of town. I've also done some Olympic games and filled in on some 76ers games. Oh, and I did one of the Russian hockey games when one of their all-star teams was playing the New York Islanders at Nassau Coliseum. The league called and asked if I could do the Wings of the Soviet against the Islanders. That's the game the Islanders lost 2–1. On one important play, Islanders goalie Glenn "Chico" Resch went to clear a puck and his stick snapped in half. The Russians ended up scoring and that keyed the win. This was the day before the Flyers famously beat the Red Army 4–1 at the Spectrum. The Red Army was the other team—and the best one—that the Russians sent as part of an eight-game, midseason exhibition tour against NHL teams.

The Islanders game against the Soviet Wings was marred by controversy. Just after the puck was dropped, someone walked down the steps and threw a plastic bag filled with red paint and marbles onto the ice. It splattered all over. People were protesting that the Russians were here, but they caught the guy and the game eventually resumed after they cleaned up the mess.

Remember the Bell?

The Bell played at old JFK Stadium in 1974, their first season, and I was paid in $1 bills to be the public-address announcer. I think they would get the money from the parking-lot workers and turn around and give some of it to the PR-type guys. I was part of Harvey Pollack's stat crew and handled the PA stuff. I was in the last row and it was hard to see, but we muddled through it. The Bell had Eagles legend Vince Papale and a bunch of guys not many people would remember.

Most of my sports memories, of course, are with the Flyers. And I can't say enough about the fans here. It may seem strange, but one of my favorite memories is the night that the hated Pittsburgh Penguins were in town and how they treated Mario Lemieux. It's something that still gives me chills and makes me proud to be a Philadelphian.

In the 1992–93 season, Mario was having one of the most incredible years in NHL history, collecting 39 goals and 104 points in his first 40 games. He then missed time because of his bout with early-stage Hodgkin's lymphoma. Mario was having radiation treatments and was unable to play in the All-Star Game in Montreal that year. I was at the game with Joe Kadlec and a few other people from our organization. Mario happened to be making an appearance in Montreal. He was still rehabbing and wasn't ready to play yet. He came out and got a big ovation at the Forum and it was nice to see.

After the game, we were flying back to Philly but we had a stopover in Pittsburgh, where Mario was headed. I was in the Montreal airport and our flight was delayed, so I took a walk and lit up a nice Cuban cigar. I walked around the terminal with my wife, and we ran into Mario, who was sitting there with his wife and kids. He was on the same flight as us. We got to talking and he said he was going to do his best to come back on the ice for the game in Philly in about a month. He had the date all mapped out.

I had known Mario because I used to go to Pittsburgh a lot on business—for my real job—and I'd stop at the arena and have a beer with the trainers after a game at the Igloo, which is what they called the old Pittsburgh Civic Arena. Mario would sneak into the training room with the trainers to hide from the writers, and I got to know him fairly well. He was always gracious, always a great guy.

So fast-forward to March 2, 1993. We were playing the Penguins at the Spectrum. I was heading to talk to the referees in their room before the game, and the Penguins were coming onto the ice for their warm-up. I saw some of our ex-players, including Rick Tocchet and Kjell Samuelsson—guys I had known pretty well who were now playing for Pittsburgh. I went over and said hello, and the last guy out of the locker room was Mario. He smiled and said to me, "Didn't I tell you I was going to play tonight?" I said, "That's outstanding."

It was such a special thing to welcome him back. When I introduced him before the game, I can remember how good I felt to announce it. He was on the ice for the opening faceoff, wearing a black collar to protect the abrasions left by the radiation treatments. He got the most heartwarming greeting—the best I've ever heard for a visitor in Philly—when he was announced. People were standing and wouldn't stop clapping. It was as if they wanted to see how long they could make it last. What a great, wonderful moment that had to be for him. I'm getting chills just thinking about it. You could tell he was embarrassed and he gave a little wave, but I know how much he appreciated it. In all his years in the NHL, he said Philly was one of his favorite visiting places to play.

Mario had a goal and an assist that night, and he finished the season with incredible numbers: 69 goals and 160 points in 60 games.

And a special place in his heart for our fans.

Philly fans are phenomenal. I'm proud of the people of Philly. This is a great fan base. Yes, there have been times when some have gotten out of hand, but we're talking about such a small percentage—and that gets blown out of proportion by the national media because, let's face it, they are trying to sensationalize things.

Stay Classy, Philly

In all my years with the Flyers, there have only been a handful of times I've had to scold the fans. One of those times came during a 2016 playoff game against the Washington Capitals at the Wells Fargo Center.

It was our first game after our iconic owner, Ed Snider, had passed away on April 11, and it naturally was a sad feeling for the fans and all of us connected with the team in one way or another. Ed was not only a great owner, but a great ambassador for the city and for hockey. His Ed Snider Youth Foundation, created in 2005, boasts over 3,000 youngsters, most of whom are from inner-city neighborhoods. The foundation's focus is on education, life skills, and, of course, hockey.

We had an emotional ceremony for Ed before the game, and fans were given light-up bracelets, which were used as part of the celebration of his wonderful life.

Unfortunately, the game was a disaster. We ended up losing 6–1 and fell into a 3–0 series hole against the Capitals, who scored five power-play goals in the game.

With 7:43 left, there was an all-out brawl and fans—unhappy with the penalties that were assessed and the fact we were facing a 4–1 deficit—heaved perhaps 100 glow-in-the-dark bracelets onto the ice.

That caused a delay, and I made an announcement over the public-address system:

"Show class…. The next one who does it will cause us a minor penalty. Do not do it!"

A short time later, more bracelets were thrown after Alex Ovechkin put the Caps ahead 5–1 by scoring a power-play goal with 5:02 to go.

A delay of game penalty was called on the fans.

"Way to go!" I yelled, sarcastically.

Inquirer columnist Mike Sielski criticized the wrongdoers for validating the worst stereotypes others have about Philadelphia sports fans.

Wrote Sielski: "They embarrassed themselves, all of them, in every possible way. When spectators scream during a pregame moment of silence for a team's patriarch—as several Flyers fans did Monday—and it's not the most graceless, dishonorable episode of the night, that's telling."

Fans and observers jumped on Twitter to share their collective thoughts.

Tweeted WIP's Marc Farzetta: "From yelling during a moment of silence to throwing bracelets on the ice…. Move over Santa, we have hit a new low."

The *Courier-Post*'s Dave Isaac tweeted similar sentiments: "The display from fans in the third period should be plenty of ammunition to give national columnists against Philly for a couple decades."

As I have said, Philadelphia fans are the greatest in the world. But that night, a handful of them created an embarrassing moment for the city.

It's important to note that not many fans threw the bracelets. Most of the fans were respectful. Frustrated, but respectful.

"We have more guys out there putting their bodies on the line, trying to block shots," right winger Wayne Simmonds said. "And it could have ultimately ended in an injury. Luckily, it didn't. It's not like we're not going out there giving an effort. Because we are going out there busting our butts."

Anyway, after we won two straight and cut Washington's series deficit to 3–2, the Flyers printed orange T-shirts for Game 6 at the Wells Fargo Center. The shirts, given to fans who attended the game, had my caricature on it, along with the phrase STAY CLASSY PHILLY!

At first, I was a little embarrassed when I heard about the T-shirts, but I was honored that they did it.

The night the bracelets were thrown, I was especially aggravated because it came on the night that Ed Snider was honored. We should have been thinking about that as well as the game; we shouldn't have been thinking about negative things.

But, again, it was less than one half of 1 percent who threw the bracelets. I don't know where they came from, but they were unthinking fans, and as I said at the time, if they want to visit with me in the penalty box, they can come on down. They know where I am.

The next day, the team released a statement, calling their fans the "best in sports," but expressing regret over what happened during Game 3.

"Flyers fans have the right to voice their displeasure vocally or by not watching or attending games, but when displeasure is expressed in a way that embarrasses or endangers others," the statement read, "it cannot be condoned or tolerated."

Signing one of my STAY CLASSY PHILLY T-shirts after an incident at a playoff game earlier in a 2016 series against the Washington Capitals.

I think Ed Snider's daughter, Sarena, said it best with a tweet she sent the day after the incident.

"My dad would've called the wristband throwers a 'disgrace' & may have spoken publicly," she said. "But he wouldn't look back, only forward."

An epilogue: we gave out bracelets at our 2016–17 home opener and no one threw any on the ice. That was nice to see, though we lost the game to Anaheim 3–2.

Rubbing Elbows with the Famous

Being part of historic and heartwarming moments—like Mario Lemieux's return—is one of the perks of my job as public address announcer.

Another perk: being around some high-profile people, such as Sylvester Stallone, Donald Trump, Sarah Palin, and Peter Jennings, just to name a handful.

At the 1993 All-Star Game in Montreal, I got to meet Jennings, a Toronto native who was the popular news anchor for *ABC World News Tonight.* Anyway, I was in our Four Seasons hotel lobby one afternoon and I saw Peter and his family. I went over and introduced myself and told him I worked for the Flyers. He shook my hand and we made small talk. I asked him if he was going to the All-Star Game that night. He told me he was trying to work that out, and I said, "Why don't you come over in the NHL bus with us? You can sit next to me." He said, "That would be great." So now I have Peter Jennings in my pocket and I figured I'd have some fun with it.

All our execs were staying at the Four Seasons, and later that evening, they were all getting on the bus to take them to the game. I got on the bus last with Peter Jennings and I started introducing him to our guys. I remember saying, 'Peter, do you know our owner, Ed Snider?' They shook hands and started talking and then Peter sat down next to me and we had a nice long chat like we'd known each other our whole lives. The truth of the matter is that we'd known each other for maybe five minutes. But what a great guy. He was as easygoing in person as he was on TV. Very approachable and not full of himself.

Later that night, Ed Snider came up to me and said, "How the hell do you know Peter Jennings?" And I told him the truth. I said, "I don't." So I told him the whole story.

"Lou, you are unbelievable," Snider said.

By the way, that All-Star Game, which was the last one ever played at the old Montreal Forum, wasn't as memorable as the conversation I had with Jennings. The Wales Conference defeated the Campbell Conference 16–6. What I remember most about that game was the heartfelt tribute given to Lemieux before the game. He wasn't able to play because of treatments he was receiving for his illness, but he was able to attend.

Mike Gartner of the New York Rangers scored four goals for the Wales and was named the game's MVP, and Mark Recchi, who was the Flyers' lone representative, chipped in with a goal for the winners.

Snider Boots Trump

As for Donald Trump, Ed had invited him as his guest and they sat in Ed's box together and watched a game at the Spectrum. Before the game was over, Ed told him to leave the box because he was talking too much and Ed couldn't concentrate on what was happening on the ice.

Who knew that one day Trump would become president of the United States?

Anyway, I approached Trump at the game that night. I just wanted to say hello and shake his hand. He's a luminary. He's Donald Trump. But I never got near him. As soon as I made a move toward him, he was cordoned off by a couple of his bodyguards. Trump moved in a cocoon, even back then. I never got to talk to him, but that's okay. Right now, if he was sitting a few feet away from me, I'd probably let him sit there and wouldn't have much interest in him.

Palin (Not Poulin) in the House

I didn't talk to Sarah Palin, either, when the Republican vice presidential candidate came to the Wells Fargo Center (then known as the Wachovia Center) to drop the puck before our 2008–09 season opener. I got to introduce her, but it was difficult to get close to her. Between the bomb-sniffing dogs and the Secret Service guys and the wanding, there were a lot of safety precautions being taken that night. They had an area underneath the arena—where the guys play soccer to loosen up before each hockey game—that was blocked off with drapes and poles, and no one was allowed back there except her entourage. They had couches and tables set up for her and her group. I remember announcing her as America's No. 1 hockey mom, and they booed the hell out of her. It wasn't very pleasant, but she didn't seem to care.

Ed Snider, who was a Republican, claimed he didn't invite Palin as a political candidate but said she was there because she "meant so much to hockey and was a hockey mom."

Bill Daly, the NHL deputy commissioner, echoed Ed's comments. In a statement, Daly said, "We do not view the Flyers' invitation to Governor Palin to be politically motivated."

The fans, however, didn't see it that way. The *Philadelphia Inquirer* did an online poll that received 8,323 responses, with 63.8 percent saying they didn't like the idea of Palin appearing at the game, and 36.2 percent saying they favored it.

Palin dropped the ceremonial first puck between Mike Richards and the Rangers' Scott Gomez. The Alaska governor then took a tour of the building during the first period and asked to stop by the Flyers locker room, where she wrote a message on the dry-erase board: LET'S GO BOYS!

It didn't inspire us. We lost 4–3 and dropped our first six games (0–3–3) to start the season. Some folks in the media called it the Palin Curse.

Meeting "Rocky Balboa"

I got to meet Rocky Balboa—uh, I mean, Sylvester Stallone—after a game at the Spectrum in the late 1970s.

He is a very nice man—very gracious.

My mom and stepdad, Gus Andersch, had season tickets for a while and they were at a game that Sly attended. Gus' son, Roy, used to hang with Sly growing up in the same neighborhood in Philly. So Gus knew Stallone pretty well when Sly was younger.

Sly went into our locker room after the game to talk to our guys, and I brought Gus down to wait in the hallway. I said to Sly, "My stepfather's outside the room, and he's from Palethorp Street." I caught him off guard. He said, "Palethorp Street?!" It was like a light went on in his head and he was a little kid again. For a moment, he probably started remembering about all fun they had in the neighborhood. He asked me who was waiting for him outside the locker room. When I told him it was Gus Andersch, Sly got all excited and said, "Let's go find him." So he was reunited with Gus, and it was pretty cool. They had a good time talking about the old days.

Sly enjoyed meeting the players that night, but I think he even got a bigger kick out of seeing Gus again. It was the first time they had seen each other since long before *Rocky*, and long before Sly became famous in Hollywood.

Remembering the Spectrum

Some of my favorite memories are from the Spectrum. Not just because we won a Stanley Cup there, but because that was where we played when our franchise was born in 1967.

In a way, the Spectrum was like my second home. I was 21 when I started working there, so I grew up in that building. It was a sad day when we played our last game there—an exhibition—in 2008. There were a flood of memories that came back to me, including my first game as a PA announcer after replacing Kevin Johnson. To be frank, I was scared to death.

But I got through it, and my nerves calmed down after that. I've had a lot of crazy stuff happen down there. The first several years I did it, there was no glass around my box and I'd get hit with sticks and pucks all the time. I was always getting dinked. I remember one time I talked to Bob Kelly before a game and he said, "Louie, I'm gonna put someone in your lap today." Sure enough, he checked a guy and he fell right into my lap and all the scoreboard buttons went off—and the scoreboard went crazy.

Thanks, Hound.

In all my years with the Flyers, I probably missed only 6 to 10 games, most because of my broker duties.

One of the games I missed was on December 8, 1987. That was the game in which Ron Hextall became the first goalie in NHL history to shoot the puck and score a goal. John McAdams was my replacement that night, and he loved to bust on me about it.

Hexy was one of the NHL's best puck-handlers among goalies; it was almost like he was an extra defenseman out there. So when Boston pulled goalie Reggie Lemelin—who had been drafted by us 13 years earlier—and added an extra attacker late in the game, it wasn't surprising to see Ron control a loose puck, tee it up, and loft in high toward Boston's end. It landed near the Bruins' goal line and rolled into the empty net.

"It was a perfect opportunity for me with us being up two goals at the time," Hextall told reporters after the game. "I looked up and saw the open ice. I was hoping to get the puck close. I shot it and saw it roll in. It's a great feeling."

Not for those of us who are usually there...but missed that game!

The goal, scored at 18:48 of the third period, put Philadelphia up 5–2 on the Boston Bruins in front of a capacity Spectrum crowd.

But at least I was at the Spectrum for the biggest goal in Flyers history. The Spectrum was in a frenzy that afternoon when I announced: Flyers goal scored by No. 19, Rick MacLeish. Assist, No. 6, Andre Dupont.

It was a simple 13-word announcement that, looking back on it, became a franchise-turning moment. It was the only goal scored in that game against the Boston Bruins, and it forever made the Spectrum known as the House that Clarke Built.

That day—May 19, 1974—is etched into my memory. The Spectrum was wired from before the start of the game. There was anticipation that this was going to be a very special day, and you could feel the electricity crackling in the air. It was a tight, hard-fought game and, with us clinging to a 1–0 lead, the noise level in the third period was astounding. Remember, this was only our seventh season in the league. An expansion team wasn't supposed to be this good so quickly.

With 2:22 left in the game, Boston's legendary defenseman Bobby Orr was called for pulling down Bobby Clarke. Holding was the penalty, and when Orr came to the penalty box, he couldn't believe the call. I mean, he was incredulous. He was livid because he knew it almost assured us of winning the game and the Stanley Cup.

A little later, as the clock wound down, I wanted to announce "Last minute of play to the Stanley Cup!"

I didn't, of course. It wouldn't have been professional, and I didn't want to jinx it. Can you imagine if I had made that announcement and the Bruins had tied it and then won the game? I would have been the most hated man in Philadelphia!

Truth be told, when I did announce it was last minute of play, I don't think anybody heard me. The place was going bonkers. The noise level was through the roof. It was probably the most famous game ever played at the Spectrum, a magical building that saw its share of special moments.

To this day, I proudly wear a ring that has the Flyers logo with the words REMEMBER THE SPECTRUM on it. One side of the ring has the arena engraved on it, and the other side has my name on it.

I also wear a team ring that I saw Freddy Shero wearing before we won our first Cup. He put me in touch with the rep who was selling them. I'm glad he did, because it's an important keepsake to me.

God Bless Kate Smith

One of the most popular nonplayers to ever step on the Spectrum ice was the great Kate Smith, who became the Flyers' good-luck charm.

Kate made four personal appearances at the Spectrum, and the Flyers would play a recording of her "God Bless America" if it was an important game. Our record when the song was played: 100–29–5 heading into the 2016–17 season. I will talk more about Kate and the amazing effect she had on our franchise in a later chapter.

I will say this: Kate became connected to the Flyers because club vice president Lou Scheinfeld was upset by the lack of respect some fans were showing during the national anthem. So Lou became rebellious himself.

Many fans at Flyers and 76ers games were "apathetic or rude" when the national anthem was played, Scheinfeld said. Some refused to stand. Some talked while the song was being played.

"I wanted to get their attention," Scheinfeld said.

Enter Kate Smith's recording of "God Bless America."

The rest, as they say, is history.

CHAPTER 6

LASTING IMPRESSIONS: PATRIOTISM OVER PUCKS

During my long association with the Flyers and around other sports, I have witnessed some remarkable moments. And some sad ones. Here are the ones that were the most impressionable:

- Our win over Boston that gave us the 1974 Stanley Cup
- With the rest of the NHL actually rooting for us, jolting the Russian Red Army in 1976
- The game following Pelle Lindbergh's tragic death in 1985
- Working the Olympic Games in Salt Lake City in 2002
- President George W. Bush's live address to the nation that was shown on our scoreboard to fans at one of our 2001 exhibition games, nine nights after 9/11
- Handing the public-address duties at the NCAA Frozen Four Final in 2014 and watching future Flyers defenseman Shayne Gostisbehere have a goal, two assists and a plus-7 rating, leading tiny Union to a 7–4 win over Minnesota

By conservative estimate, I have witnessed close to 3,000 hockey games in person in the last 50 years. Many of those games have faded from the memory bank. Oh, they were exciting at the time, but they didn't leave a lasting impression.

You can probably guess the game that left the biggest impression. It was May 19, 1974, and the Spectrum was percolating on that unforgettable Sunday afternoon. That was day we outlasted the favored Boston Bruins 1–0 and stunned the experts, capturing the Stanley Cup in six games—and in just our seventh season after the franchise was formed.

Our win over the Russian Red Army in 1976 ranks as the No. 2 highlight of my career, but you may be surprised at another game I rate high (fifth, to be exact) on my list. And it wasn't even a "real" game. It was an exhibition contest in 2001 against the New York Rangers. And the game, oddly enough, was never completed.

The exhibition was played at the Wells Fargo Center, which was then known as the First Union Center, on September 20, 2001.

You could tell right from the start that the atmosphere was different. The game was played nine nights after the 9/11 attacks, and miniature American flags were handed out to fans as they entered the arena. The First Union's new 360-degree LED video board, which wrapped around the upper-deck railing, displayed red, white, and blue bunting.

There was an extraordinary scene before the game as the Philadelphia firefighters and police, showing their appreciation and respect for the relief efforts after 9/11, walked to center ice and unfurled two American flags. The US Marine color guard also joined the group, and the Flyers and Rangers, in a sign of solidarity, skated to center ice and stood side by side during Lauren Hart's a cappella version of "God Bless America."

Just retelling the story now gives me goose bumps. It was a proud night for all of us, a night I will always remember.

Chants of "USA, USA, USA" echoed around the First Union Center before the game started, and you could feel the brotherhood of the 14,000 or so who were in the building.

Late in the second period of a brawl-filled game, the Flyers' Mark Recchi tied the score at 2–2, and a few minutes later, the teams went to their dressing rooms for the second intermission.

During the intermission, President Bush's national address to Congress about the terrorist attacks was shown on the Jumbotron, beginning about eight minutes before the scheduled start of the third period. But when the players skated back on the ice to get ready for the third period, a message on the screen said the game was about to resume and that the remainder of Bush's speech would be shown on the monitors in the concourse.

The fans began booing.

"Leave it on! Leave it on!" they chanted.

That prompted Ron Ryan, the Flyers chief operating officer, to order that Bush's address be put back on the Jumbotron. The game was put on hold. For the next 33 minutes, the players and fans watched the speech. The players were on their benches, and they tapped their sticks on the boards—as if giving their applause—to certain portions of the speech.

"We did what the fans wanted," Ed Snider, the Flyers' chairman, said of returning Bush to the Jumbotron.

Snider and Ryan decided to call off the third period, and the exhibition game thus ended in a 2–2 stalemate. I announced the game was ending in a tie because of respect for the United States and in support of the president's speech.

During the speech, the fans cheered loudly when Bush vowed to eliminate terrorist groups and to bring to justice those responsible for the 9/11 attacks. The cheers grew louder when Bush named Pennsylvania governor Tom Ridge to head his new office of Homeland Security.

The fans even put aside their hatred for New York on this night. They cheered when New York City mayor Rudy Giuliani and New York governor George Pataki were shown on the screen.

When the game was called, players from both sides agreed with the decision.

"We get paid to play this game because the people want to watch us," said Rangers defenseman Brian Leetch, who lost a close college friend in the World Trade Center collapse, "but they made it clear what they wanted to watch."

"The right decision was made," Flyers coach Bill Barber said, adding that Bush's speech exceeded "any sporting event."

"I lost sight that I was in a hockey game," Flyers forward Keith Primeau admitted.

Flyers forward Jeremy Roenick said the players felt a bond with the fans.

"I was more impressed watching it with 13,000 or 14,000 people," he said. "How can you play hockey after that?"

In addition, the players would have been at risk of an injury had they resumed the third period after such a lengthy delay. When the game finally was called, there was another development that raised the goose-bump count: the teams lined up at center ice and shook hands.

It was a beautiful gesture, a show of unity and respect after the teams had been involved in six fights and had combined for 112 penalty minutes in the first two periods.

In short, it was a special night—a night of patriotism, togetherness, and healing. A night that made you proud to be an American.

Where Were You on May 19, 1974?

To baby boomers who are Flyers fans, May 19, 1974 has special significance. It always will.

Even the kids of baby boomers are probably familiar with the story: that was the date the Flyers defeated the Big, Bad Bruins 1–0 and won their first Stanley Cup.

Winning a Cup for the first time is special in its own right. Winning it just seven years after the franchise's creation, well, that's downright amazing. The headline on the front page of the *Philadelphia Inquirer* the next day started with: MIRACLE FLYERS. That's how stunning it seemed at the time.

We were clinging to a 1–0 lead—Rick MacLeish tipped in a point drive by Andre "Moose" Dupont in the opening period—as the final minutes ticked away. The Bruins would not go away without a fight.

You knew they were going to come at us because of their pride. Then it got down to five minutes left, and three minutes left and you started saying to yourself, "This might really happen."

The Bruins had a great scoring chance with just under three minutes to go as Ken Hodge took a pass in full stride and fired a ticketed shot from about 10 feet above the right circle. The blast was no more than six inches off the ice and was headed just inside the far post.

But the 17,007 fans in the building exhaled as Bernie Parent kicked the puck away, starting a fastbreak down the other end.

Bill Barber retrieved the rebound and fed Terry Crisp, who sent Clarkie away on what would have been a breakaway if Bobby Orr had not caught him from behind and grabbed his arm.

Just 2:22 was left, and Orr was given a two-minute holding penalty by referee Art Skov. Orr was absolutely fuming, yelling at the ref and calling him every single name you can call a guy. But the fact is, if he didn't grab him, I think Clarkie would have been in alone.

From the time he got in the box until the end of the penalty, Orr did nothing but berate the ref.

The Bruins lost two precious minutes of potential offense, and they were cooked. As the final seconds ticked away, Gene Hart's broadcast became legendary: "Ladies and gentlemen, the Flyers are going to win the Stanley Cup! The Flyers win the Stanley Cup! The Flyers win the Stanley Cup! The Flyers have won the Stanley Cup!"

As I mentioned earlier, I didn't do anything differently. I didn't grandstand and make a big deal when there was a minute left. You don't want to say, "Last minute of play until the Stanley Cup!"—and then the Bruins score and you're screwed. So I just played it straight. Come to think of it, when I announced that it was the last minute of play, I don't think anybody heard it. The place was so loud. Everybody was going bonkers. Everybody was standing. Everybody was screaming.

After the game, I announced that Bernie Parent had won the Conn Smythe Trophy as the best player in the playoffs, but there was a lot of chaos on the ice. League president Clarence Campbell, who did not like our style of play, presented us with the Cup, and I recall a photo of him at the time and he looked like he had gas. He was not a fan of the Orange and Black.

Meanwhile, hundreds of fans had climbed over the boards and joined in the celebration as Bernie and Clarkie tried to skate around with the Cup. I can remember Schultzy (Dave Schultz) running interference for them, pushing fans out of the way so they could make their way around the ice.

Do I think the fans ruined the celebration? Not really. They participated in it, maybe a little more than they should have. But the Stanley Cup celebrations in those days were a lot different than they are now. Now it's all scripted. Back then, the glass was a lot lower and fans could get over it fairly easily. That wouldn't happen now.

Maybe the fans climbing onto the ice cut the celebration a little short because the Cup couldn't be handed off to too many people. There was too much congestion on the ice for that. But the fans were caught up in the moment. I'll bet there are 40,000 people who claim they were on the ice after that game when, in fact, there were probably 500, 600, or so.

Me (right) with Flyers accountant Ralph Hawthorne after winning the Stanley Cup in 1974. I'm wearing my trademark orange Flyers blazer.

There was craziness in the locker room as the players were joined by their parents and their wives or girlfriends. It was packed. I remember Clarke, being asked about his party plans, said that he would just follow his goaltender. "I'll walk across the water with Bernie," he said.

I had a blast that day. I got some photos taken with the Cup and drank from it. I had to stick around because I was doing the PA for the Philadelphia Wings' indoor lacrosse game that night. Weeks earlier, Fitz Dixon, who was one of the Flyers' owners at that point, had asked me to do the Wings games and I had agreed. Little did I expect that their first game would be the night we won the Stanley Cup!

I had a lot of drinks after we won the Cup, and my hair was still sticky from champagne. I did the Wings game while I was still wearing my orange Flyers blazer. After the Wings game, I got to

Rexy's, the Flyers hangout in South Jersey, and joined the players. They were still going strong and we partied until they closed the bar.

It's a wonder my head doesn't still hurt.

Bring on the Russians

As I mentioned, our victory over the Russian Red Army team in 1976 ranks high on my personal list of all-time favorite games that I worked.

The Red Army was Russia's top team. The Soviets' No. 2 team, the Wings, was also powerful and also was playing NHL teams.

At stake was the NHL's credibility.

No NHL team had been able to beat the Red Army during the tour, so it was up to the Flyers to save the league's face. How ironic. The NHL bigwigs despised the Flyers because of their brawling, intimidating style. Suddenly the league was pulling for the Orange and Black.

Clarkie said we were the NHL's "last stand," and he was right.

We had to win the hockey game or it would have set our league back for a while. As it turned out, we set the Russians back instead.

I was working at PSFS Bank at that time. I took a couple days off and went to practice to get a feel for the Red Army. I remember how badly the room smelled. It was brutal. Anyway, their captain, Boris Mikhailov, came out and handed me a Russian pin with their logo. I said thanks. He wanted something in return. I signaled that I had nothing, but I went through my pockets. I had a Kennedy half dollar and I gave it to him. He seemed very happy with it. I went into the hallway and was talking to somebody and, a couple minutes later, the locker room door opens and Mikhailov points to me. And this group of Russian players all came over to me and gave me pins, thinking I'd give them a Kennedy half dollar in return. I got the interpreter and explained to them that I would get the coins for them but I had to go to the bank to get more. I went to PSFS, my bank, and got a couple rolls of Kennedy halves and got more pins in exchange. You would have thought they struck gold because they were so happy with the trade.

It was interesting to watch the practices because they had a bunch of KGB agents watching them, making sure they didn't defect. And one of the agents took all the Kennedy half dollars away from the players. They weren't allowed to keep them. Back in the days of the Cold War, Kennedy and Khrushchev weren't exactly on good terms, so I guess the agent thought it was insulting for them to have the half dollars. But later on, I managed to give some of their players some more Kennedy halves. I wonder if they ever made it home.

But the sideshow aside, the game, played on January 11, 1976, at the Spectrum lived up to its billing. We were the two-time defending Stanley Cup champions at the time, and the Red Army wanted to show they could beat the NHL's best. The hype for that game was incredible. I remember Fred Shero saying he couldn't wait for the game. He had gone to Russia and incorporated some of the Russians' techniques to the Flyers' game and he was anxious to see the results.

Freddy was a very pensive guy and was way ahead of his time in a lot of aspects. I was fortunate in that once on a train from Montreal to Toronto I spent most of the night in Freddy's compartment, drinking beers with him and Joe Kadlec and Frank Udvari, the supervisor of NHL officials and a former referee. Just hearing Freddy talk about the intricacies of the game and seeing how excited and passionate he was, well, it really left an impression on me. I was a young kid in my twenties at the time, and I was loved hearing Freddy's stories and seeing what made him tick.

Freddy's strategy for that game was simple: hit the Russians early and often and throw them off their game. With 8:39 left in a scoreless first period, one of our veteran defensemen, Ed Van Impe, charged out of the penalty box and dropped Valeri Kharlamov with an elbow to the head. Kharlamov fell to the ice, facedown.

Later, Van Impe said Kharlamov "ran into my elbow." His tongue, of course, was firmly in his cheek.

The Red Army was furious at Van Impe's hit and by the Flyers' physical nature. Russian coach Konstantin Loktev argued with the officials, and when he wasn't satisfied with the results, he ordered his team to retreat to the locker room.

"We have never played [against] such animal hockey," Loktev said.

Flyers owner Ed Snider, stunned at the developments, headed downstairs and met with NHL president Clarence Campbell and Alan Eagleson, executive director of the NHL Players' Association.

Lloyd Gilmour was the referee. The Russians gathered at their bench and Gilmore went over there. Aggie Kukulowicz was Air Canada's rep, and he spoke Russian. He was the interpreter in the middle of things and he was the liaison between the Russian coach and the referee. Gilmore came over and asked Aggie, 'What do you think we should do here?' Aggie told Gilmour that they were just trying to intimidate him. Gilmour agreed and gave them a two-minute penalty for delaying the game. He held up two fingers for the penalty. The Red Army thought *they* should have been getting a power play because of the hit, and it turned out they were going to be short-handed, so they decided to head to their locker room.

When Snider learned the Russians had not yet been paid for this game or for some others in the series, he devised a plan. Through an interpreter, the Russians were informed they would not get paid if they didn't return to the ice.

They came back.

When play resumed, we dominated. The Russians became more passive, and their walkout seemed to inspire our players and give them more focus. We finished with a dominant 49 to 13 shots and whipped the Russians 4–1 as Reggie Leach, Rick MacLeish, Joe Watson, and Larry Goodenough scored for the Flyers.

Watson, a solid defenseman, wasn't exactly known for his scoring, and he went crazy when he scored the goal. You would have thought we had just won the Stanley Cup! To this day, the guys still bust on Joe about that goal. They tell him that when he scored, he set the Russians back a decade.

Ed Snider proudly kept the front page of the Russian newspaper from the next day. In Chuck Gormley's *Orange, Black & Blue*, Snider said the newspaper showed "big behemoths with Flyers logos beating the Russian players with big clubs. I can't tell you how much I love that cartoon."

Getting the Olympic Call

One of my biggest thrills was getting invited to do the public address work for the 2002 Olympic hockey games. That would rank high on my list of most memorable live events.

I was the English-language men's announcer in Provo, located about 40 miles outside of Salt Lake City. It was different. There was no paper or script for me to read. You read everything off a computer screen. I did work one women's game, an exhibition game between

Belarus and China. I was reading the Chinese names and the French announcer was talking to me in English through my headset. He kept saying, 'Hey, Louie, they're looking at you! They're looking at you!' So I figure if they're looking at me, something must be wrong. All the players were standing on the blue line and they're supposed to acknowledge when their name is called. Well, it turns out the computer information I was given had the names backward, so I was reading their surname first and their first name last. We straightened that out and got the pronunciations down pat—and in the right order. But other than that, things went rather smoothly.

That was the year that Canada defeated the U.S. 5–2 in the men's hockey final. Joe Sakic and Jarome Iginla scored two goals each to lead Canada. I didn't do that game because I did the games in the smaller venue. I did the US and Canada in some of their other games, but not in the one that determined the gold medal. In fact, when I did a Canada game, Eric Lindros got a penalty and he came in and sat in the penalty box and he looked up and asked me, "What are you doing here?" I smiled and said, "I just announced your name. Didn't you recognize it?" He said he wasn't really paying close attention and didn't realize it was me.

The games were very competitive in that Olympics. The US team had a lot of older players. Chris Chelios was 40, Brett Hull and Phil Housley were 37, Tom Barrasso was 36, and Mike Richter was 35. And we had a lot of guys in their early thirties, including Johnny LeClair, Brian Leetch, Jeremy Roenick, Bill Guerin, Mike Modano, and Tony Amonte.

The Canadian team was a little younger and had the Flyers' Simon Gagne, who was just 21. Lindros, who was 28 and in his first year with the Rangers, was on the Canadian team. Canada had guys such as

Mario Lemieux, who was 36 but still had two goals and four assists, and Stevie Yzerman.

I did every team at one time or another, and it was a great experience. I had a blast. There were a lot of extra security measures taken that year because it wasn't too far removed from 9/11. About six weeks before the Games started, I remember flying to Utah with a group of people—all kinds of different nationalities—to familiarize ourselves with the layout of the arenas. They told us they were going to lock the plane down 30 minutes into the flight and no one was going to be allowed to get up. I was sitting next to a lady and started talking to her and it turned out she was a federal agent. She had a list of the other agents who were on the plane and carried a firearm. There were 10 or 12 of them.

And the arenas had lots of extra protection. It was a little bit inconvenient, but you got used to it and no one complained. I think everybody understood the reason for it, and it made everyone feel safe once you went through the metal detectors and were inside.

I did the PA work and I also did previews of the hockey games that were shown on the arena scoreboard. We read through the stats and just gave the basics on what to look for.

I was thrilled and honored to be a part of the Olympics; it had been a long journey to get there.

The first hockey games I ever did were at the Cherry Hill Arena for the Jersey Devils. This was during the '60s, and I filled in for a handful of games. The Devils played in the Eastern Hockey League. The players were not very disciplined and the referees weren't the best either. Lots of fights, lots of penalty minutes, lots of craziness. There was a lot of stick work going on in the Eastern League.

Getting to the Olympics made me smile and think back to those long-ago days with the Devils. It's been quite a journey for a guy from Southwest Philly.

Trying to Follow Pelle

The game that is third on my most memorable list is a matchup that most Flyers dreaded playing. It was November 14, 1985, the first game after Pelle Lindbergh's death.

It was memorable because of the emotions that boiled over. The fans, players, and everyone involved with the team were still in a state of shock at Pelle's death from an alcohol-related car accident in Somerdale, New Jersey. Pelle was driving when his Porsche crashed into a three-and-a-half-foot high wall in front of an elementary school.

Pelle was so popular with his teammates and the fans; he was a guy who everybody thought would take us to our next series of Cups. And just like that, he was gone.

Two nights after Pelle died, we faced the Edmonton Oilers at the Spectrum. The Flyers politely declined Edmonton's offer to postpone the game.

"We've got to start sometime," said Clarke, the team's general manager. "We've got to learn to live with what happened."

It was an empty feeling that night. Just a very somber atmosphere. No laughing, not much talking, not a lot of anything. Just an existence. The players came in and did what needed to be done.

Before the game, a memorial ceremony was held at the Spectrum, giving the fans a chance to say good-bye. In an eerie coincidence, Pelle's picture had been printed on the tickets for that game against Edmonton. Fans were also given a small picture of the goalie, and someone unfurled a sign from the upper level: GET PELLE'S NAME ON THE CUP. IT'S HIS LAST CHANCE.

The building was darkened and a wreath of flowers forming Pelle's No. 31 jersey was placed at center ice. It was a very subdued crowd, but there were big cheers when our players came onto the ice. The people stood and applauded for a minute or so. It was like they were saying, "We'll help you get through this, and you'll help *us* get through this." It was terrible for everybody.

Several speakers talked about Pelle, including broadcaster Gene Hart, who said we were not mourning Pelle's death but celebrating his life, one that we "were privileged to share." The ceremony lasted 23 minutes, and the little Swedish goalie was recalled as someone who loved life.

Then we went out and beat the powerful Oilers 5–3 to register our 11th straight victory. As the players skated off the ice, the fans gave them an emotional standing ovation.

Afterward, Mike Keenan said winning the game was nice, but irrelevant. "I'm just so proud of the way they played," he said.

Because of an injury to Bob Froese, rookie goalie Darren Jensen was thrust into action after being recalled from the minors the previous day.

"I had all sorts of butterflies," Jensen said, "but once the game started, I thought about hockey."

With all the emotion swirling around the building, it was amazing that we played as well as we did that night. Pelle would have been proud.

Seeing a Ghost

On a much more upbeat note, watching defenseman Shayne Gostisbehere for the first time is also on my list of most memorable games.

This was in the NCAA's Frozen Four at the Wells Fargo Center in 2014. I did the public address announcing and got my initial glimpse at the player they call Ghost, who was selected by the Flyers in the third round of 2012 draft. (We picked center Scott Laughton in the first round and goalie Anthony Stolarz in the second.)

I had heard a lot about him, but never did I expect to see him be so dominant. He had a goal, two assists and a staggering plus-7 rating to lead tiny Union to a 7–4 win over Minnesota in the championship game.

Think about that: plus-7. That means he was on the ice for all seven of his team's goals and was not on the ice for any of Minnesota's four goals. Amazing. It was absolutely unreal that someone could be plus-7 in a pressure-packed NCAA championship game.

The guy was so effortless in the way he did things in that game. That's been brought to our attention now because we've had a chance to see him play in the NHL with the Flyers, but he really jumped out at you in that game. This, of course, was before he became one of the top rookies in the NHL in 2015–16 and finished second in Calder voting.

I remember getting excited watching him orchestrate that win over Minnesota and seeing him take over the game. I was thinking to myself, *This is* our *guy.* It's amazing that he lasted until the 78th overall selection. Give our scouting people and then–general manager Paul Holmgren credit for making a very shrewd pick.

Ghost put Union on the map in that game, giving the Dutchmen their first national hockey title. You are forgiven if you had never heard of the school before Gostisbehere and his teammates worked their magic. The school, located in Schenectady, New York, didn't become Division I in hockey until 1991–92 and didn't have a winning season until 2007–08.

I also got to meet Boston College's diminutive winger, Johnny Gaudreau, at the 2014 Frozen Four. During the tourney, it was announced that he had won the Hobey Baker Award as college hockey's best player. Gaudreau, a South Jersey native who attended Gloucester Catholic High, has become an NHL All-Star with the Calgary Flames. Like the Ghost, he was drafted relatively late (fourth round of the 2011 draft) and has shown that he was actually worthy of being a first-rounder.

Gaudreau won the Hobey Baker Award a day after his team lost to Union 5–4 in the NCAA semifinals. Nicknamed "Johnny Hockey," he had a goal and two assists in that game—and he finished the season with 36 goals and 80 points in 40 games.

I introduced myself to Johnny and he said, "I know who you are. I used to come to Flyers games." I hear Johnny would love to return to the East Coast some day. Who knows? Maybe one day he'll be playing for the team he used to root for when he was growing up.

It's great to see a local guy make it, and Johnny Hockey has certainly made the region proud.

When I was growing up in Southwest Philly, I played baseball and football for local teams. In football, I was an interior lineman and a kicker. I picked No. 76 because it was the number Lou Groza wore for the Cleveland Browns. I was a big fan of Groza, who was one of the top NFL kickers.

I later switched to No. 60 after another one of my heroes, Chuck Bednarik, an Eagles two-way star who played a big part in their 1960 championship. He was a linebacker and center, one of the league's last two-way players, and was a devastating tackler. I loved Chuck and the way he played, and I got to meet him a few times in later years. He was grand marshal of a parade in Jim Thorpe, Pennsylvania, a sleepy town named after the great all-around athlete. They also had me in the parade as a celebrity, though I never did think of myself as one.

ABC's Wide World of Sports named Thorpe the top athlete of the 20th century, and they had a big ceremony where he is buried. They also had a huge parade to celebrate Thorpe being honored as the century's best athlete. Everybody was out in their lawn chairs and it was a big deal.

I was a big sports fan growing up. I loved the Phillies. I started following them in the '50s when they had guys such as Granny Hamner, Stan Lopata, Del Ennis, Andy Seminick—I loved catchers because I caught a lot back in the day—and, of course, Richie Ashburn and Robin Roberts.

In the summer, we'd play baseball all day. We'd leave in the house at 8:30 in the morning with our taped bats, and we'd have balls wrapped in tape because the covers would get knocked off. We played in a vacant lot near 60th Street, below Lindbergh Boulevard. We played there all the time, and at Finnegan's Playground on 70th and Lindbergh. We played from dawn to dusk, coming home only for lunch and then going back. Nobody ever worried where we were. Things were different than now. Now everybody is driven to their games and you can only pitch a certain amount of innings in Little League. Things weren't as organized back then, but that may have been better. We had a ball. We also played lots of hockey on roller skates at St. Barnabus, my grade school. Very informal. We got chalk and outlined a net. High-tech stuff.

My dad died when I was nine, so sports was a big outlet for me. Kind of an escape. Playing sports kept me occupied, as did following the big-league teams, including the Ramblers, who had guys like Billy Kurtz, Ray Crew, and Rocky Rukavina on their Eastern League team. Joe Kadlec was their stickboy. After the Ramblers games ended, they allowed you on the ice, so that's where I learned to skate a little bit. I wasn't very good at it, but I had loads of fun. The Ramblers played at the Arena, near 46th and Market Street, and they had a big marquee outside—it looked like a movie marquee—that told you who they were playing.

I'd watch the Game of the Week on TV, and that's where I got to know names like Bobby Hull, Stan Mikita, and Glenn Hall. And later on, I got to meet all these guys, so it worked out pretty well.

I was also a big Eagles fan as a kid. Pete Retzlaff and Tommy McDonald were the guys I really liked, along with Norm Van Brocklin and Concrete Charlie (the great Chuck Bednarik). I saw the Eagles' championship win over the Packers at Franklin Field in 1960. It was bedlam. I guess it was a precursor to us winning Stanley Cups.

It's hard to believe that the Eagles haven't won it all since that 1960 game.

I wasn't good at basketball, but I liked going to Warriors games growing up. We used to sneak into Convention Hall. We'd pay the guy a buck and he'd let us run upstairs and we got to see Wilt Chamberlain in action. Back then, football was my favorite sport, baseball was second, hockey third, and basketball fourth. Hockey was only third because we just had a minor-league team and you didn't have a chance to see many NHL games on TV. But hockey obviously soon vaulted to No. 1 for me.

Mom Was the "Anchor"

Growing up, my mom was really the anchor of our family after my dad died. My dad was a blue-collar guy who fixed oil burners, and my mom was a stay-at-home mom. That was typical of families in the '50s and '60s. Most moms stayed at home and ran the household. My mom was a big influence on me, as were a lot of teachers I had along the way. So was Joe Kadlec, our first public relations director. Joe always had class about him with the way he dealt with people in general. When we went on the road, *everybody* knew Joe because of the kind way he treated people. I remember one time we got off a bus in Montreal and we went through the boiler room. There was a guy working and he said, "Hey, Joe Kadlec! How are you doing, my friend?" Joe was friends with everybody—from a boiler-room guy to the president of a hockey team. He treated everybody with class and respect. Joe just had a way with people and still does. He's one of my greatest friends.

I think Joe's contributions to those Stanley Cup teams don't receive as much credit as they should. He bent over backward for those guys—from getting tickets to making sure everybody was happy. Whatever they needed, he'd say, "No problem."

Getting back to my mom, after my dad died, she went to work as an administrator for an insurance company. She met my stepdad at work; he fixed and did maintenance on elevators.

In a strange coincidence, years later that's where I met my wife—I started talking to her in an elevator when I worked at PSFS Bank. I'd had my eye on Ellen for a while; she was an architect at PSFS, and I was a teller. I quickly became a supervisor and then sold bank services to businesses.

I would always flirt with her, but she would never give me the time of day. I later found out she really couldn't see what I was doing. She was vain about wearing glasses and would always take them off, so she never saw me making a fool of myself. One day we happened to be in an elevator together, and I told her I had been trying to meet her for a couple months. I asked her to lunch. It was the start of something wonderful.

Me and my wonderful wife, Ellen.

CHAPTER 7
IN MY HUMBLE OPINION...

When picking an all-time Flyers team, you have to start with Bobby Clarke, Bernie Parent, and Bill Barber. That's the easy part. After that, it gets a little tricky.

Based on my 50 years with the club, I'm going to give you my list of the franchise's top players, coaches, and general managers, along with the guys who are my favorites in the penalty box. Since I sit between the penalty boxes, I have some amusing stories. A lot goes on down there that the cameras don't always catch.

First, here are my all-time Flyers teams for the first 50 years—and, believe me, some of the decisions were not easy:

First Team

(All stats are for games with the Flyers only)

Left winger: Bill Barber
Stats: 903 games, 420 goals, 463 assists, 883 points, plus-316 rating
Years with Flyers: 1972–73 to 1983–84

Center: Bobby Clarke
Stats: 1,144 games, 358 goals, 852 assists, 1,210 points, plus-506 rating
Years with Flyers: 1969–70 to 1983–84

Right Winger: Reggie Leach
Stats: 606 games, 306 goals, 208 assists, 514 points, plus-212 rating
Years with Flyers: 1974–75 to 1981–82

Defense: Mark Howe
Stats: 594 games, 138 goals, 342 assists, 480 points, plus-349 rating
Years with Flyers: 1982–83 to 1991–92

Defense: Eric Desjardins
Stats: 738 games, 93 goals, 303 assists, 396 points, plus-143 rating
Years with Flyers: 1994–95 to 2005–06

Goalie: Bernie Parent
Stats: 232–141–104 record, 2.42 goals-against average, 50 shutouts
Years with Flyers: 1967–68 to 1970–71; 1973–74 to 1978–79

Coach: Fred Shero
Stats: 308–151–95 record (.642), 48–35 playoff record (.578), won two Stanley Cups
Years with Flyers: 1971–72 to 1977–78

General Manager: Keith Allen
Stats: 563–322–194 record (.612), won two Stanley Cups, reached the Finals four times
Years with Flyers: 1969–1970 to 1982–83 (Note: Before becoming the GM, Keith was the first coach in our history.)

Second Team
Left winger: John LeClair
Stats: 649 games, 333 goals, 310 assists, 643 points, plus-197 rating
Years with Flyers: 1994–95 to 2003–04

Center: Eric Lindros
Stats: 486 games, 290 goals, 369 assists, 659 points, plus-188 rating
Years with Flyers: 1992–93 to 1999–2000

Right winger: Tim Kerr
Stats: 601 games, 363 goals, 287 assists, 650 points, plus-90 rating
Years with Flyers: 1980–81 to 1990–91

Defense: Jimmy Watson
Stats: 613 games, 38 goals, 148 assists, 186 points, plus-295 rating
Years with Flyers: 1972–73 to 1981–82

Defense: Joe Watson
Stats: 746 games, 36 goals, 162 assists, 198 points, plus-191 rating
Years with Flyers: 1967–68 to 1977–78

Goalie: Ron Hextall
Stats: 240–172–58 record, 2.91 goals-against average, .895 save percentage, 18 shutouts
Years with Flyers: 1986–87 to 1990–91 and 1994–95 to 1998–99

Coach: Mike Keenan
Stats: 190–102–28 record (.638), 32–25 in playoffs (.561)
Years with Flyers: 1984–85 to 1987–88

General Manager: Bud Poile
Stats: He had just a 56–78–43 record, but he set the franchise's foundation with his excellence in the expansion draft, and he later took a gamble on a diabetic named Bobby Clarke in the second-round of the 1969 draft
Years with Flyers: 1967–68 to early in 1969–70

There were challenges to picking the teams, but goalie was easy. Bernie Parent was not only a great Flyer; he was one of the best goalies of all time. He played back in the days of the standup goalie, back when they had much smaller equipment. Bernie had such great reflexes and he would have been a star no matter what era he played in. The bigger the game, the better he played. He had nerves of steel.

Joe Watson, one of our defensemen, tells the story about Bernie calling him over with four minutes to play in the deciding game of the 1974 Stanley Cup Final. Joe thought Bernie was going to have a serious discussion, but that wasn't Bernie's style. Bernie said, "I'll bet there are a lot of broads watching us right now." Bernie was just trying to keep Joe loose because Joe was a very high-strung guy.

Bernie won two Conn Smythe Trophies, awarded to the best playoff performer each year, for leading us to Cups, and was named to the Hall of Fame. If I don't pick Bernie, people would be questioning my sanity.

My defensemen in front of Bernie would be Mark Howe and Eric Desjardins. Howe was so dependable, and he could go up ice when he had to. He scored a bunch of big goals for us, and one season (1985–86) he was plus-85. Just think about that.

Desjardins was great every game. Very consistent. He could make any play, and to this day he is still the best I have ever seen at keeping the puck in at the point along the boards. It seemed like he was never out of position, and if somebody rammed the puck around the boards to get it out of the zone, Rico was there to keep it in—whether it was his stick, his hands, or his body.

There were a couple guys pretty close to Rico, but I give him the overall edge.

As for the forwards, Clarke would have to be my center. Like Bernie, he's a no-brainer. He was the best player to ever put on the

Orange and Black, and his intensity was second to none. He would kill you to win. And he did not take well to losing or to having penalties called against him. As I said earlier, I don't think there's one penalty he thought he ever deserved.

Clarkie was relentless and nobody outworked him, but he also had a lot of talent. Nobody could dish the puck like him. He knew where to put it and when to put it on a teammate's stick. He played with wingers that scored a lot of goals—guys like Bill Barber, Reggie Leach, and Bill Flett—and they didn't just get the puck all by themselves and run it up the ice. Nobody could make passes like Clarkie.

Barber and Leach are my all-time Flyers wingers.

Barber was a great all-around player who played in every circumstance—penalty kill, power play, even strength—and he was terrific in every area. He had an excellent shot and was hard to take off the puck, and he had enough speed to get past someone and create a scoring chance.

I am going with Reggie Leach as the right winger, which means my all-time top players were the same ones that formed the famed LCB line—Leach, Clarke, and Barber. I didn't go in with the intention of picking an actual line that was intact when it played, but it just turned out that way.

Reggie had a killer of a shot. Maybe he wasn't here quite as long as some of the other players I have on the list, but he had so much to do with our success here. He had 45 goals during his first year with us and was a big part of our 1975 Cup, then had 61 goals in his second year and won the Conn Smythe as the top player in the playoffs in 1976, the year we lost to Montreal in the Finals. That year, he had an incredible 19 goals in 16 playoff games.

Reggie was just a scoring machine, and the chemistry he had with his old buddy, Clarke, was something to see.

Interestingly, only two of the 12 players on my all-time first and second teams played for the Flyers beyond 2000: Desjardins and LeClair.

Six of my top 12 players played on at least one of our Stanley Cup teams, and my picks as the franchise's best coach and general manager were also from those days. That's why I chuckle when people say we won the 1974 and 1975 Cups because we were goons. No, we won because we had tons of talent, grit, a great coach, and a shrewd general manager.

My second-team goalie would be Ron Hextall. He led some great teams, starting with the 1986–87 squad, when he came in as a rookie and took us all the way to the Finals, where we lost to a great Edmonton team in seven games. Hexy was so dominating he was named the Conn Smythe winner.

Besides his outstanding play, I loved Hexy's competitiveness and his leadership. I considered selecting Pelle Lindbergh as the No. 2 goalie in franchise history. Pelle was great and getting better, but unfortunately he only played in 157 games with the Flyers before his tragic death. If Pelle had been here longer, he may have been No. 2 on the all-time list. As it stands, I would have him as our third-best goalie in history.

On defense, Jimmy Watson is one of the guys I have on the second team. And I probably surprised some people with my selection of his brother, Joe Watson, as his defensive partner. I considered Kimmo Timonen, Brad McCrimmon, and Chris Pronger—Prongs, to me, wasn't here long enough to earn a spot on one of our all-time teams—but I went with Joe Watson.

Joe was an underrated player. He was a very steady defender and one of the best leaders we've had. It was tough putting him ahead of Kimmo Timonen—a great player in his own right—but Joe had a way of bringing the team together. And the fact that Joe was one of our top defensive players when we had our greatest success, well, that counts for something.

Jimmy Watson was so steady at both ends of the ice. And he came in and established himself right away—he was a rookie in 1973–74, when we won our first Cup—and it didn't seem like he had much of a learning curve. He was so consistent and never missed a responsibility on defense, and he was one of the few guys on our blue line who could carry the puck down the other end. He was a complete player and a leader back there.

On the second-team front line, I picked John LeClair over Brian Propp, and, believe me, it wasn't an easy choice. They both scored big goals. I think Proppy was probably a more well-rounded player than John, but John was just so dominating and he used his size to shake off opponents and create a lot of chances by himself. He was so strong on the puck. John would camp out in front and you couldn't move him out of there, and he drew a ton of penalties because opponents became frustrated trying to contain him.

LeClair came here in a trade with Montreal—one of the best in Flyers history—and he made an immediate impact. I remember Clarke, our GM at the time, saying that Eric Desjardins was the guy they really wanted in the deal. They also wanted LeClair, of course, and the deal could not have worked out better for us. We traded top-line right winger Mark Recchi to the Canadiens for Desjardins, LeClair and second-line winger Gilbert Dionne.

Dionne became a bust, but it didn't matter. We ended up getting two of the greatest players in our history.

Props to Clarkie.

LeClair could not have fit better on what became known as our Legion of Doom line, with Lindros and Mikael Renberg.

Lindros is the center on my second all-time Flyers team, ahead of such great players as Rick MacLeish and Dave Poulin. Eric made passes that other players could not make, and in a lot of instances, LeClair was the recipient, slamming those things in.

Eric revolutionized the game. Until he came along, the NHL had not seen a player of his size who could also play with such finesse when it was needed.

My second-team right wing is Tim Kerr. He was another guy who took a beating, day in and day out, but he got it done. He was such a big, strong player. He was part of a great line, with Poulin and Propp—one of the best lines we've ever had.

Rick Tocchet was another great right wing, but I put Kerr ahead of him. Timmy was just so consistent. During one four-season run, he had 54, 54, 58, and 58 goals. Enough said.

Fred Shero gets my nod as the best coach in Flyers history, ahead of Mike Keenan.

Freddy is a no-brainer. He was an innovator who was ahead of time. He was not afraid to think outside the box. He went to Russia and learned things from their game. And Freddy got results. His record was outstanding, and he was the mastermind behind our two Stanley Cups.

It's worth mentioning that Freddy was also a great motivator. And he kept the players on their toes because they could not figure him out. There's a story the guys tell me about Freddy coaching in the minors. The day after his team won 10–2 he had them skate for more than 1½ hours. He just sat in the penalty box, smoking a cigarette and blowing a whistle. He was punishing them with a hard skate because he didn't like what they did the previous night. Even though they won by a lopsided margin, he thought they had been too freewheeling.

Freddy was different, and I mean that with all due respect. He just liked to be alone and do his own thing. But he was always a step ahead of everybody. Always thinking about what he could do to get the most out of his players.

As I said, Freddy liked to think out of the box. Like Game 6 of the 1974 Stanley Cup Finals against the Bruins and the great Bobby Orr. What does Freddy do? He tells his players not to keep the puck away from Orr but to let him have it at every opportunity and keep hitting him. By the end of the game, Orr was gassed. It worked.

Keenan was another coach who got a lot out of his players. I originally picked Keith Allen as my second-team coach, but after a lot of thought, decided to select Keenan. Keith was our first coach and he set the tone for the franchise. But he only coached for two years before moving upstairs to become the GM.

Keenan was here four years, and we made the playoffs each season and twice reached the Finals. Wherever he has been, he has been a contentious coach and not necessarily well-liked by his players. That said, he knew how to get the most out of them and a lot of young players developed under his watch. He was demanding and he got results.

You always wonder if the direction of the franchise would have been different if Pelle had been around. Keenan was the coach when Pelle died in the car accident. Maybe if Pelle had been here, we would have won a Cup or two and Keenan would have ended up staying in Philly for a much longer time. That's not to take anything away from Hextall. He did a great job after he, in effect, replaced Pelle a year later. But it's only natural to wonder "what if?"

Pat Quinn is another guy I considered as the all-time second-team coach. He was a very likable guy, and he coached us during our

35-game unbeaten streak, highlighting his 3½ years here. He took us to the Finals in one season. Great person, great coach.

As for general managers, Allen stands at No. 1. He built two Cup champs and made a ton of spectacular trades.

The second-best general manager is a tougher decision, but I went with Bud Poile.

Poile, our first GM, was a passionate guy and he also did a great job. His expansion draft—he picked guys like Joe Watson, Gary Dornhoefer, Ed Van Impe, and Bernie Parent—put the franchise in motion. And he drafted Bobby Clarke in 1969 when a lot of teams shied away because of his diabetes. He also drafted Dave Schultz and Don Saleski, two key wingers on our Cup teams. In addition, Poile named Allen as our first coach, and that was an excellent hire.

As a GM, Clarke deserves special mention because three of his teams reached the Stanley Cup Finals.

Ron Hextall, our current general manager, has shed a lot of salary cap and made some shrewd draft picks, so he is off to an impressive start. I wouldn't be surprised if Hexy ends up moving to No. 2 on the list of top GMs. Time will tell.

We've had only seven different men as general managers in 50 years, so that's one position that hasn't had a lot of changes in our history.

As for the two all-time teams I've picked, I'm sure a lot of people disagree with some of my choices, but that's what makes picking these teams so much fun. They create conversation, and that's the main reason for doing them. There have been so many great players in our 50 years here, and you are bound to leave off some terrific guys—players like Simon Gagne and Rick MacLeish, and on and on.

My All-Chatty Team

In the last 50 years, I've spent a lot of time next to the penalty boxes and have heard a lot of interesting chatter.

Just for the fun of it, here's my most talkative Flyers team (penalty-box division): Joe Watson, Zac Rinaldo, Ryan White, Wayne Simmonds, Jeremy Roenick, Keith Jones, Jake Voracek, Rick Tocchet, Craig Berube, Orest Kindrachuk, Brayden Schenn, and Luke Schenn.

Dave Schultz spent 1,386 minutes in the penalty box in just four seasons with the Flyers, and when he got to the box he was generally still boiling. He wasn't the kind of guy I could have a conversation with because he was usually still fuming from a fight he just got into. Dave still had that intensity when he came to the box.

Clarkie wouldn't talk much to us when he got to the box, but he certainly never stopped talking to the referees, linesmen, or opponent. (And he never thought he deserved a penalty.) He never thought he was guilty...but, most of the time, he was guilty.

It's funny how you remember different things about players. I remember Zac Rinaldo always wanted some chocolate when he was in the penalty box. He'd ask me or the penalty-box guy if we had any. We usually had some down there.

One of the best guys to deal with was Ryan White. I was sorry to see him go—he signed as a free agent with Arizona after the 2015–16 season—because he always had a good word for us. No matter what he went through—whether he beat somebody up or was beaten up—he always had good words when he came to the box. He'd say, "Hey, guys, how are you?" Sometimes guys had to cool off at the beginning of a penalty, but Whitey was always cordial. He took time to get to know everybody's names and he always had respect for people doing their jobs—as we did for him doing his.

Everybody has a different demeanor when they get to the penalty box. Some need some time to cool off before they're themselves. Simmonds is usually very intense when he gets to the box, yelling a lot at the ref. Voracek is more chilled out when he gets to the box. Different players, different personalities.

Keith Jones was a laugh riot when he got to the box. No different than he is now on the radio. He'd always have a wise-guy comment, always ready with a one-liner.

As for opponents, I always enjoyed Rob Ray, Matthew Barnaby, and Tie Domi. They usually were in the penalty box for a while because of fights. I remember one time Rob Ray was absolutely cleaned up in a fight by the Fridge, Todd Fedoruk. He came in and asked if anybody had a cell phone he could borrow.

"Cell phone? Why do you need a cell phone?" I asked.

"I want to call Matt Barnaby," Ray said.

"Why's that?"

"I want to tell him that the Fridge is left-handed so he has a better chance against him," Ray responded.

Ray was great. Never took himself too seriously. And Barnaby was a lot of fun, too. He'd always agitate the fans. That was part of his M.O. Barnaby was a great guy. For my son Matt's bar mitzvah, I took my camera around and made a video, asking people to wish him a great day. I had a whole bunch of different guys on the video—referees, Zamboni guys, players. And Matt Barnaby was one of the guys who was gracious enough to do it. He did it while he was in the penalty box. He said, "Hey, Matt, have a great day! You have a great name, I'm sure you know!"

The players were very kind. Clarkie got on there and said, "Okay, Matt, you're a man now. Make sure you have your dad take you out for a beer." I even had Arlen Specter, the Pennsylvania senator, wish Matt a happy bar mitzvah from the Wing Bowl, which is an annual eating contest (among other things) that is held at the Wells Fargo Center. I also do some announcing there and bring some customers and we have a great time.

Some people will probably be surprised when I call Tie Domi a great guy because he was Public Enemy No. 1 in Philadelphia when he played for the Toronto Maple Leafs.

Flyers fans will always remember what happened at our rink on the infamous night of March 29, 2001.

Domi had gone to the penalty box, where he was being taunted by a fan. Domi didn't like it and, in an act of immaturity, he reached over the glass and squirted the fan with a bottle of water. Twice. The fan didn't back down. He leaned on the glass, which broke, and all of a sudden, he tumbled into the penalty box and was in there with his new pal, Domi.

The two exchanged punches, and Domi even pulled the fan's shirt over his head as he slugged away, before being separated by linesman Kevin Collins. The fan—a 36-year-old concrete worker named Chris Falcone of Havertown—suffered a deep cut on his forehead.

"They threw stuff at me. Once was enough," Domi told reporters at the time. "After the second one, I told the guy [worker] in the penalty box that after one more, I was going to squirt water...I didn't plan on fighting."

In 2015, 14 years after the incident, Domi and Falcone were on the *WIP Morning Show* and were reunited on the phone.

Domi called Falcone a great guy.

"How you doing?" he asked.

In the interview, Domi was asked how the two men patched up their differences that night.

"We solved it like two street guys," Domi said. "No lawyers, no nothing. We shook on it."

Domi went on to explain that he paid for Falcone to come to Toronto for two playoff games with his family.

"I put you up here. Everything is good now," he said to Falcone. "I'm really glad it worked out....You're a great guy and a family guy, and I'm happy everything is behind us."

"You, too, man," Falcone said. "You, too."

Domi retired in 2006, but he said he still gets fan mail from Philly. "More than any place in the whole league, to tell you the truth," he said, adding he "played up" his antics in Philly for the fans. "They were on me and I would kind of taunt them, too, so it was a lot of fun."

Fighting Tips

I mentioned Ray saying he was going to give Barnaby tips on how to fight Fedoruk. Well, things like that aren't uncommon in the NHL.

Flyers winger Riley Cote, for instance, thanked Georges Laraque for giving him a tip after Cote lost a fight to him. That happens a lot when young guys are trying to build a reputation; they'll pick a fight with somebody and thank them after for going with them.

I remember when Cote went with Laraque—a guy who was really tough. When they were finished, Laraque must have told him how he got inside him and was able to get some punches in. So when they got to the box and both got their breath back, Riley said, "Georges, thanks for the fight and thanks for the tips. I appreciate it." They're tough guys, but they're gentlemen.

Intensity Is Their Calling Card

Any conversation about the most intense Flyers players of all time would have to start with Bobby Clarke.

But you may be surprised at my list of players who played for the Flyers and displayed the most intensity from the penalty box.

Defenseman Nick Schultz would be somewhere on that list. He never stops talking or directing his teammates when he's in the penalty box. He gets in the box, and for his whole two minutes he's standing up, encouraging his teammates, telling them when they are

The Flyers first line (left to right)—Claude Giroux, Jakub Voracek, and Scott Hartnell—all next to me in the penalty box.

skating into trouble. He is constantly coaching his teammates. Mark Streit was like a coach in there, too.

Michael Del Zotto is likewise always shouting out at his teammates.

Claude Giroux is fairly quiet in the penalty box. He doesn't say much unless he has to. If he has a question, he'll ask me. He might ask, "Can you get that replay up again?" if he didn't see it the first time. Something of that nature. I don't put up the replays myself, but I can ask the Arena-vision guys to put it up again. Sometimes they have time to put it back up, sometimes they don't. If they have already put it up and play has restarted, they're usually not going to be able to put it up again. But if they can, they will help.

Speaking of Referees...

I've had some interesting conversations with referees over the years.

Take, for instance, the one I had with referee Paul Devorski a few years ago at the Wells Fargo Center.

We played a game a day or two after a concert, and some confetti leftover from the concert had collected atop the scoreboard. We scored lots of goals in this game, and every time we scored, the horn on top of the scoreboard would sound off and it would send confetti fluttering down to the ice. Not a lot of confetti, but little strips. The colored strips you could see, but the white ones blended into the ice. The officials were chasing the confetti all over the place and trying to make sure they didn't miss any of it because, obviously, it can be dangerous to anyone that is skating. So Devorski came over to me after we scored another goal and said, "Louie, if you blow that horn one more time, I'm going to give you guys a minor penalty for delay of the game."

I had one word for him: "What?!"

Now, I had a headset on, and the guy who blows the horn, Mark Wyatt, was listening to our conversation. He said, "Okay, I won't blow the horn anymore." We scored a couple after that and no one blew the horn. But can you imagine if we blew it and they gave us a penalty—in effect, for celebrating a goal in normal fashion? If that happened, Ed Snider would have had an interesting conversation with the league, and I'm not sure the NHL would have won that argument.

Don't Help the Ref!

I've had a good working relationship with virtually all the NHL referees over the years. We work hand in hand. They give me the penalties and the guilty party so I can announce them to the fans. We have mutual respect for one another.

But one thing I've learned: don't try to help out a referee. Ever. It makes him feel like he's not in charge. And referees definitely want to feel in charge.

There was one game in which there were a couple fights, and when they ended, the referee, John McCauley, came over to me to give the penalties. He was thinking about who it was that he was going to penalize, and he started thinking out loud, and I got the impression he wanted help sorting things out. He paused and seemed like he was searching for who did what. So I put my two cents in and gave him the names of the guys who were fighting.

McCauley wasn't grateful. He looked at me and seemed annoyed that I had spoken. "Louie," he said, "I'm the ref and you're the announcer. I'll referee and you announce."

I was just trying to help out! But I've learned not to volunteer things. I just sit there and wait for them. They're in charge...even when they do ask for help.

Referee John McCauley talks to me (right) at the Spectrum, back when there was no glass protecting us.

Amusing Anecdotes

I've had a front-row seat to a lot of amusing things that have happened in the penalty boxes.

One of them occurred in the 1970s at the Spectrum. Dennis O'Brien of Minnesota was sitting in the box, and one of *Sports Illustrated*'s photographers was in there. He had a couple different cameras and he had one just sitting there in the penalty box. O'Brien picked up the camera that was attached to a hockey stick and started jabbing it at Bill Barber in the other penalty box. The photo made all the national wires.

The camera guy has his mouth open like, *Oh, no. Oh, no.* I'm sure it was an expensive camera and I'm sure he thought it was about to be in 1,000 pieces. But O'Brien calmed down and the photographer quickly grabbed the camera and took it away.

The ironic thing is that the wire-service guys and the local newspapers got the best photo because of the *Sports Illustrated* photographer.

Lots of bizarre things happen down there. There was a time in the '80s Glen Cochrane, one of our hardnosed players, was in the penalty box and a different kind of commotion developed. There was no glass in front of us at that point. In our box, there was an off-ice official, me, and the timer, John Maurer, who always wore a Jeff cap that he would take off, place on his briefcase, and watch the game. He was a brush-haircut kind of guy, a no-fooling-around guy.

Well, Cochrane was in the penalty box, and one of the Flyers scored a hat trick—So the hats go flying onto the ice. Hundreds and hundreds of them. So, I got caught up in the moment and I said, "Why not?" I wanted to be a part of it. I picked up John's cap and I threw it on the ice like a Frisbee. I figured it wouldn't be a problem, because they always collect the hats and John would get it back. John saw the hat flying onto the ice but didn't see who threw it. He turned to Cochrane and said, "My hat! Why the hell did you throw my hat?!" Cochrane told him he didn't throw it, but John didn't believe him. "You just heaved it right out there!" He was livid. They got into a big argument, and they were jawing back and forth.

I confessed, and we made a phone call and made sure someone got that particular hat and returned it to John because I guess it had special meaning to him. John eventually got his hat back and I got off the hook.

Sometimes I wish the players had mics on in the penalty box, because the fans would really be entertained.

Take the time Daymond Langkow was playing here. He was an intelligent, witty guy and always had something amusing to say when he was in the penalty box. He didn't come in much, but he was a feisty guy, a lot like Danny Briere was.

One time he lost his stick while he was on the ice, and it went flying through the air and hit a guy on the other team. The ref blew the whistle and gave him two minutes. Daymond was incensed.

"Two minutes? For what?"

"You high-sticked the player."

Daymond got madder by the second.

"I didn't even have a hold of the stick!" he said. "Somebody slashed it out of my hand."

He came in and sat in the penalty box, and he was stewing. I said to him, "Well, that was interesting. How the hell did the stick go flying through the air like that?"

And he said, "Jedi mind trick."

I still can't stop laughing today when I think about his response. It didn't take him more than a half second to respond. What a classic line.

CHAPTER 8
BIZARRE MOMENTS

When your franchise has been around for a half-century, there are going to be a lot of wacky, bizarre moments that take place. We certainly have had our share.

Take the last game of the 1969–70 season. (Take it, please. And bury it and don't let it come back to haunt us ever again.)

All we needed to do was beat the lowly Minnesota North Stars in that afternoon contest to be in the playoffs, a fitting reward for Bobby Clarke's rookie year. Clarkie had a modest 15 goals and 46 points, but you could see he was going to be something special.

You had to feel good about our chances in that regular-season finale. Earlier that season, the North Stars had just one win in a 34-game stretch. Hard to do.

It was a defensive struggle, as Bernie Parent and Minnesota goalie Gump Worsley were locked on a scoreless tie heading into the third period. With about 12 minutes left, the unthinkable happened: a North Stars rookie named Barry Gibbs—a name that would live in Flyers infamy—lobbed a shot from a little beyond center ice. As Jay Greenberg wrote in *Full Spectrum*, the shot "floated toward the goal like a watch dangling from a hypnotist's hand."

Time was about to run out on our season.

Bernie didn't see the puck at first. He then made a sudden but late move toward his right, but the puck was past him. The North Stars had a 1–0 lead.

Some accounts said Bernie lost the puck from the afternoon sun that had been streaming through the windows. But Bernie said someone stepped in front of him and he lost the puck for an instant.

"It happens sometimes," he said.

I can still hear the painful groan from the crowd after Gibbs scored.

It ended up being the game's only goal. We lost 1–0. We had nothing to show for a long, grueling season.

Bernie allowed just 18 goals in his last 10 games, but everyone would remember the one that got past him at that critical juncture. It was our sixth straight loss, five of them by one goal. We scored a total of just 12 goals in our last 10 games, which was the main reason we won only one of them.

Gibbs just dumped it into the zone and I think the North Stars were making a line change, and poor Bernie is still looking for it. After that, they put black curtains up near the entrances and into the seating area so the sun couldn't shine in during day games. (But, again, Bernie didn't use that as an excuse.)

And it just so happened that the fan club had planned their annual party for that night. The players always attended and it started out *really* quiet before it got rolling and people realized you couldn't change things. That put a bit of a pall on the party, at a restaurant on the water—Walber's on the Delaware in Essington. Not far from the building. Right past the airport.

Between Gibbs' goal and the one scored by Chicago's Patrick Kane that beat us in the 2010 Stanley Cup Finals, you would think there couldn't possibly be another score that was as painful.

But I'll give you another example of a Goal That Shouldn't Have Been Scored, and I think you'll agree it was just as haunting.

Two years after Gibbs' improbable score, we again were knocked out of a playoff spot by giving up a third-period goal on the last day of the regular season.

This time, it was Buffalo's Gerry Meehan who did the honors. That's another name that lives in Flyers infamy.

Longtime Flyers fans remember what Meehan did to us, but the previous game gets lost in the shuffle. We blew a 4–2 lead to the Penguins in that game, and Pittsburgh tied it after pulling its goalie in the final minute. That missed point would cost us dearly.

We went into the final game, in Buffalo, knowing we needed one point to guarantee a playoff spot. Just like the game in Pittsburgh, we had a two-goal lead.

Do you detect a pattern here?

The Sabres eventually tied the game at 2–2 on Rene Robert's goal with about 11 minutes left in the third period. It would remain tied as we headed into the waning minutes. On the radio, an excited Gene Hart was counting down the time that needed to elapse before the Flyers were in the playoffs.

And then Meehan, a former Flyer, skated over the blue line and ripped a 45-foot shot toward our goalie, Doug Favell. Favy kicked out his left leg and lunged with his glove.

The puck whizzed past him. Four seconds remained. The Sabres had a 3–2 win. Our season, incredibly, was over.

Favy later said he cried knowing he had let down the team.

Our first-year head coach, Fred Shero, searched hard for the right words when asked how he felt when Meehan's shot hit the back of the net.

"The same way I did when my mother and father died," he said.

Those early years were filled with heartache, but that just made what happened in 1974 and 1975 even more special. We survived the tough times—two unfathomable losses that knocked us out of the playoffs on the last day of the season—and lived to tell how it had strengthened our focus and resolve.

Oh, the Pane

There have been an inordinate amount of oddball occurrences in our franchise's history.

Another one that comes to mind: A late-season game in the 1992–93 season.

Outside, a blinding snow was piling up, making driving conditions treacherous on that March 13th day.

It was almost spring, but our area was getting hit by something called a snowicane—heavy snow combined with hurricane-like wind gusts over a short period of time.

Inside the Spectrum, it was decided that the show would go on. We were hosting Wayne Gretzky and the Los Angeles Kings in a matinee.

That was the plan, but the game was stopped after the opening period.

The blizzard dropped more than a foot of heavy snow on the area, making it difficult for the players—most of whom lived in South Jersey—to drive to the Spectrum. Some of the players, including Eric Lindros and Kevin Dineen, stopped along the way to help people push their cars that had gotten stuck in the snow.

There might have been 2,000 people at the game, and during the first period I became very popular by making an announcement and inviting everybody to come down to the expensive seats on the first level.

Loud cheers echoed around the building.

With about two minutes left in the first period, however, the cheers turned to groans. The relentless snow and high winds caused a large pane of glass to shatter onto the concourse. Thankfully—and miraculously—no one was seriously injured. We were very fortunate that the game was going on at the time and people were in their seats. There were concession stands right below the window that blew out, and if it had been between periods, there would have been a long line there—and it could have been a disaster, with lots of serious injuries.

There was a big boom and glass was everywhere, and it even went flying into parts of the stands. The last two minutes of the first period were played, and the teams then left the ice tied at 1–1.

After the period ended, the coaches, the three officials, and club president Jay Snider huddled, and the fire marshal said the building was unsafe. It was decided that in order to protect the fans, the game would be postponed. Weather reports said the storm was intensifying—the snow would be followed by several hours of heavy sleet—and that also played a part in the decision.

I made the announcement that the game was going to be postponed, and I think everybody understood. They were more concerned with how they were going to get home, because the snow was piling up. I remember talking to Gretzky in the hallway to the locker room after the game was called. It was one of the few times you could talk to him without him being surrounded by a whole group of people. Later on, when he was with the Rangers, it always seemed like he had an entourage whisking him up and down the hallways. But on that day, I think everybody's defenses were down and everybody felt like one of the guys, I guess. Human nature left everybody humbled, and guys from both teams were just hanging out in the hallway and talking to each another about what had happened.

I drove to our home in Penn Valley and I couldn't get down my street because the snow was so high. I live on a cul-de-sac and I ended up parking around the corner in a church lot—apparently it had been plowed for church the next day—and then walked home.

In case you were curious, 19 days after that postponement, the game was replayed in its entirety on April 1. The Kings won 3–1 and Gretzky had a pair of assists.

And Who Can Forget...?

If you were at the Spectrum on December 18, 1993, you undoubtedly haven't forgotten what transpired.

We were playing the Blackhawks and we received a delayed penalty, giving us an extra attacker. That should be a good thing, right?

Uh, well, 99.999 percent of the time.

We had pulled our goaltender, Tommy Soderstrom, to put an extra skater on the ice. We had the puck in Chicago's defensive end and seemed to have it set up pretty well when Garry Galley, from near the goal line, slid a puck back to the point to Kevin Dineen.

Oops. The pass went wide of Dineen and the puck headed down the ice...toward our unguarded net. I can still hear the reaction from the fans. It was like the play was in slow motion and you could hear everybody trying to will the puck to go wide.

"No. Nooooo. Nooooooo."

The fans were pleading for the puck to miss the net.

It didn't.

After the puck went in, it seemed like the air went out of the building, like someone hit the mute button. The groans were replaced by stunned silence.

The fluke shorthanded goal gave Chicago a 2–1 lead.

But Yves Racine scored a power-play goal just 45 seconds later, allowing us to salvage a 2–2 tie.

Best Goalie Fight Ever

I've probably witnessed thousands of fights during my career with the Flyers, and a few stick out, including the pummeling Dave Schultz gave to Dale Rolfe in Game 7 of the Stanley Cup semifinals in 1974. No Rangers came to help Rolfe, and the fight seemed to take the life out of their team.

Another fight that sticks out: Felix Potvin vs. Ron Hextall on November 10, 1996, at the Wells Fargo Center, which was then known as the (brand-spanking-new) CoreStates Center. Goalie vs. Goalie. They must have thrown 20-some punches apiece. It's known as probably the greatest fight ever between goalies.

Goalie fights are rare. They have so much bulky equipment that it makes it difficult to throw punches.

That said, Hexy and Potvin didn't have any problems. It was the Frazier–Ali of goaltender fights.

The Hockey News ranks it as the best goalie fight in NHL history, and it's difficult to argue with the assessment. Google the video when you get a chance. It's worth a look.

We had a 3–1 lead as the final buzzer sounded and Potvin slashed at Daniel Lacroix as he skated past him. Wendel Clark, one of the Maple Leafs' tough guys, then went at it with Lacroix. That's when Hextall bolted from the net, skated the length of the ice, and charged into the Toronto zone.

Potvin and Hexy had not spoken any angry words beforehand. But Hexy was dying to be a part of the action. Potvin had no choice but to join the fray.

"I remember looking up and seeing him coming down the ice," Potvin, nicknamed "the Cat," told the *Toronto Star*. "I was trying to get my gloves off in time. I wasn't sure what to expect."

Potvin grew up admiring feisty New York Islanders goalie Billy Smith, but had never been in an NHL fight until his bout with Hextall. But he had fought on the junior level, so he knew how to defend himself.

Hexy, on the other hand, was a combatant goalie who had fighting experience.

The fight started with the normal jostling as they tried to get position on each other. Potvin's mask came off. So did Hextall's.

It was game on.

The goalies landed numerous punches, and the strange thing was that, as the fight dragged on, players from both teams began watching the bout.

Grab your popcorn, boys. We've got a main event going.

Those games with Toronto back in the day were wild. They had a team that was mean—and entertaining, to say the least.

Hexy took a shot to the face, and that just angered him more. *Boom, boom, boom.* He fired back. They both took a *ton* of punches. Potvin didn't have the reach that Hexy did. It was as good a fight as you could see, and the fans were going crazy. They loved every minute of it.

Potvin was able to pull Hextall's jersey over his head, but they both kept flailing away until fatigue set in. After making an adjustment with his jersey, Hexy was able to throw several right hands at Potvin, who then counterattacked vigorously.

The fans stood and screamed their lungs out. Old. Time. Hockey.

"The only thing I remember is being dead tired," Potvin said. "At the end, we were holding each other and just trying to catch our breath."

According to a fan poll conducted by hockeyfights.com, Hextall was the winner. But that doesn't take anything away from Potvin. He hung right in there and even bloodied Hexy's face.

Years later, the goaltenders joked about the fight.

"I'm just happy I came out of that okay and I played the next game," Potvin told the *Star*. "My teammates were all happy that I didn't get killed."

Late in the 2016–17 season, Hextall, now the Flyers' cerebral general manager, was asked what he remembered about the fight.

"He slashed Danny Lacroix. That's what it was about. I didn't like it," he said. "It was a good fight."

Asked if he had talked to Potvin since the bout, Hextall smiled.

"I'm still looking for him," he joked.

There were a handful of goalies who didn't back down from a fight.

Billy Smith was an agitator and a tough guy and one of the better goalie fighters. Some of the bigger guys would hang on, like Casare Maniago of the old Minnesota North Stars. Patrick Roy could throw them pretty good, and Hexy was one of the better ones because he was so aggressive. He would be in attack mode by the time he got there, and not many people came to him to fight. He went to them to fight. So by the time he arrived, he was going 50 miles per hour and attacked.

As far as goalie fighters, Ray Emery may have been the king of the cowboys. He had a mean streak in him and he laid it on Braden Holtby in a 2013 fight. Holtby had no shot. Ray might have been one of the toughest goalies ever.

We were embarrassed by the Capitals that night 7–0. Early in the third period of that game our frustrations boiled over, and Wayne Simmonds and Washington's Tom Wilson went at it. While that fight was going on, Emery skated down the other end and went after Holtby, who wanted no part of the fight. Ray boxed in the off-season, so you could understand why Holtby—who is now one of the NHL's premier goaltenders—didn't want to get involved.

Looking back, Ray was just trying to wake our guys up. It seemed to work. We went 7–1–2 in our next 10 games.

Kate Smith and the Flyers

One of the most intriguing developments in Flyers history is how a fading singer became as well-known as most of the hockey heroes who played here.

I'm speaking, of course, about the late, great Kate Smith.

Her recording of "God Bless America" became our good luck charm when it was played before games. We first played it on December 11, 1969, and we beat Toronto in that game 6–3. We had won just one of our previous nine games, but Kate worked her magic.

Heading into the 2016–17 season, the Flyers had a 100–29–5 record when Kate's recording was played. Hey, I don't think Scotty Bowman would have had as much success as Kate did during that span.

Playing her "God Bless America" recording was the brainchild of Lou Scheinfeld, the Flyers' vice president of business operations.

This was during the Vietnam War era, and it was a troubling time in America.

"I noticed that some people were not standing and respecting the national anthem at 76ers games and Flyers games," Scheinfeld recalled. "People were being very rude and ignorant. I thought, 'What would happen if someone took away their national anthem? Would they care?'"

So Lou started listening to different songs, trying to find an appropriate one to replace the national anthem. At a store on South Street in Philadelphia, he found a record of Kate Smith singing "God Bless America." It was the 1963 recording from Carnegie Hall.

Scheinfeld played it at the empty Spectrum one night and thought it sounded "patriotic and rousing" as he listened to it over the arena's sound system.

"I thought, 'If this doesn't grab the crowd's attention—and maybe inspire the Flyers—nothing will," Scheinfeld said.

So before we're playing Toronto in that 1969 game, Lou told me to announce that people should please rise for the playing of "God Bless America," sung by Kate Smith. The fans were confused. The whole crowd was buzzing. It was like, "What? What are you talking about?"

Ed Snider got up from his seat in his super box and got into Lou Scheinfeld's face. "Are you crazy? You can't do this! You can't not play the national anthem!"

Lou explained to Ed that he had told him he planned to do this.

"But I didn't think you were crazy enough to actually do it," Snider snapped between expletives.

Ed went back to his seat, and we started scoring, starting hitting, started fighting. Between periods, people are walking up the aisles near where Ed was sitting and they congratulated him on this great new song and telling him it should be our new national anthem.

By the end of the game, Ed summoned for Scheinfeld. He had changed his tune.

"You son of a bitch. I don't know how you did it, but you pulled it off," he told Scheinfeld.

That was the beginning of the Kate Smith era. In the first three years that we started using the recording, we went 19–1–1. Think about that.

It sort of became a secret cult thing, and only Lou Scheinfeld could decide when it should be played. He saved it only for important games, which made our record with Kate even more impressive. Lou would call down to me about 10 or 15 minutes before the game and tell me we were using Kate that night. I'd then call the sound booth and they would cue up the tape.

Kate's agent was reluctant for her to appear at the Spectrum, and it took some luck for us to finally land her. She made four appearances, and we were 3–1 in those games. The first time she appeared was on October 11, 1973, and we beat Toronto 2–0. Former Flyer Doug Favell was the Maple Leafs goalie that night, and he said when he saw Kate was there, "I knew we were cooked."

Kate's second Spectrum appearance was May 19, 1974. That was the day we beat the Boston Bruins 1–0 in Game 6 and won our first Stanley Cup championship. After Kate was done singing before the game, the Bruins' Bobby Orr and Phil Esposito tried to kill the jinx she seemed to put on opposing teams by shaking her hand and presenting her with roses.

Kate left the ice and said to a security guard, "Wasn't it nice of the Flyers to give me flowers?" The security guard explained to Kate that it was the Bruins, not the Flyers, who gave her the flowers. Kate was stunned. "What!?"

She picked up the roses and threw them in a trash can.

Kate made two other in-person appearances at the Spectrum: May 13, 1975, before our 4–1 Game 7 win over the New York Islanders in the Stanley Cup semifinals, and before Game 4 of the 1976 Cup Finals, a 5–3 loss to Montreal, who went on to win in four straight.

Jay Seidman, our promotion director, had worked hard to try to get Kate to appear in person at the Spectrum. In fact, we had tried for several years, but her manager didn't let it happen at that time. Scheinfeld said the manager hid the requests from her. But as fate would have it, Kate had an uncle who lived in West Philadelphia, and he was sending her newspaper clips from the *Inquirer* and *Daily News* about how she had become our good-luck charm. Kate loved it! She asked her manager if it would be possible for her to sing at the Spectrum before a game. Her manager, who reportedly had wanted

Kate to sing one of her hit songs before performing "God Bless America," confessed that the Flyers had actually been calling for her.

The manager called Scheinfeld and asked for a lot of money.

"He told me she gets $25,000 an appearance," Scheinfeld said. "He said, 'Maybe you can't afford me, but don't insult me.'"

Scheinfeld offered her $5,000.

He was told it was an insult.

"At the time, her career was on the wane. A lot of people had thought she had already retired and she wasn't in the public eye," Scheinfeld said.

Kate Smith and her agent eventually agreed to $5,000.

Scheinfeld went into Ed Snider's office and told him he had lined up Kate Smith to perform live.

"That's great," Snider said. "How much?"

Scheinfeld told him $10,000.

"Oh, my god. Ten thousand dollars! Joe Scott will kill me!" he said, referring to a man who was part of the team's ownership group. "Can we afford that?"

Snider paused.

"But it's worth it, right?"

"Yeah, it's worth it," Scheinfeld said. "And guess what? I just saved you $5,000. We can get her for $5,000."

"You son of a bitch," Snider replied.

Kate was paid $5,000 for each of her four live appearances, and it helped resurrect her career.

I introduced her a few times and I met her once. I was born in '45, so I wasn't there to see her back in the day, when she was in her prominence. I know she was an icon to people around the world when we were in World War II. I've seen lots of clips of her. She was one of the most patriotic and beloved people in the country.

Kate was a very nice lady. I met her with a whole group of people in one of the lounges in the Spectrum. I just wanted to make sure I met her, and I told her I would be introducing her. She was very happy about that, and so was I. Usually when she was going to be there it was pretty much a secret. They would sneak her in and get it done—although the Bruins knew in the 1974 Finals because they had flowers for her. Somebody tipped them off.

I'm sure she was thrilled by all the attention, because now she had the opportunity to be in the public eye again. Performers love that. They love to make music and sing, but it's the people they're doing it for that make it all worthwhile, and because of the Flyers connection, there was a whole new group of fans for her. The people in Philadelphia revered her and hung on every word of "God Bless America" and sang along. When you listen to Lauren Hart do the duet with Kate now—the production guys did a great job of putting it together—it still gives me goose bumps.

To a certain extent, Kate's career was revived by the Flyers. And she loved them. She called them "my boys." It wasn't maybe a national audience that fell in love with her, because most of the people outside of Philadelphia didn't like the Flyers at that point. But those who were still alive and kicking and had followed Kate's career from the early years had to feel good about her comeback.

In 1986, when Kate died at age 79 because of complications from diabetes, Ed Snider served as one of her pallbearers. Ed and his wife, Myrna, and Lou Scheinfeld became very friendly with Kate and would exchange gifts and cards at Christmas.

One of the most famous *Daily News* front pages is the caricature of Kate holding the Stanley Cup after our 1974 win, and the gigantic headline: GOD BLESS THE FLYERS!

Kate was a special part of the Flyers, and there's a statue of her near the Wells Fargo Center, outside of Xfinity Live. How many singers can say they have a statue of themselves that was a tribute made by one of the city's professional sports teams?

Kate was more than the Flyers' good-luck charm. Much more. She was America's Voice in her younger days. She recorded almost 3,000 songs, appeared on more than 15,000 radio broadcasts and, over the years, received more than 25 million fan letters, according to the *New York Times.*

During World War II, she repeatedly was named one of the most popular women in America.

Philadelphians understand.

Lindros Loses the "C"

One of the oddest developments in our history was when Eric Lindros was stripped of his captaincy and replaced by Eric Desjardins late in the 1999–2000 season.

Sadly, there was always a contentious relationship between management and Eric. So when he came out and sniped at the medical guys—the doctor, the trainers—it created friction. Eric criticized the medical staff for not properly diagnosing him with concussion symptoms.

He was sidelined with a concussion in early March 2000 and then didn't return until Game 6 of the Eastern Conference finals. While he was out of the lineup, the "C" was taken away from him.

At the time, Bob Clarke, our general manager, said the move was *not* in retaliation for Lindros questioning the medical treatment he received after being injured on March 4.

But Clarkie was clearly peeved. He said that "when a guy like Lindros comes out and criticizes the doctors and trainers, he's thinking of himself and not the team."

He added, "We're trying to do what's right for the team" when the "C" was stripped from Eric.

Clarke met with several veteran Flyers and that they suggested appointing a captain. Eric was sidelined with a Grade II concussion after of a hit from Boston's Hal Gill.

Eric was a gamer. He always wanted to be the No. 1 guy, the best of everything. He arrived here never having played a game in the minors and there were guys taking shots at him like crazy. He would drop his gloves and beat the hell out of a guy. But as time went by, I think he was encouraged not to take the five-minute majors. They wanted him on the ice.

There was obviously some uneasiness in the locker room when the "C" was taken away from him, especially among equipment guys and trainers. Think about that. If he's going to be sniping at doctors and the medical training staff, and then he has to work with them, it's natural that the uneasiness is there. But it's in the room, and I'm not in the room.

Desjardins had all the tools to be the captain, but I believe he felt uneasy about it. It had to be uncomfortable to get the captaincy with all the controversy swirling around the situation. I don't think he wanted it, but it was matter of "you were an alternate captain, and now you're the 'C.'" A nicer guy than Rico didn't exist. And what a player. He was one of the best defensemen we've ever had, probably second only to the great Mark Howe.

The epilogue to this messy time in Flyers history is that Lindros was a trailblazer for today's players. Back then, I don't think there was any medical protocol or rules for concussions. Those rules weren't in place until much later. In a way, Eric brought awareness to the situation, and today players have to go through concussion protocol before they are allowed back on the ice.

Happy Halloween

Since this chapter focuses on unusual but memorable developments, I couldn't leave out Jeremy Roenick.

J.R. is one of the best American-born hockey players in NHL history. He was also one of the game's most gregarious players and was a fan favorite when he played for us from 2001–02 to 2003–04.

He scored some big goals, but one of the first things I think of when you mention him is his Bobby Clarke impersonation during warm-ups before a 2001 game.

Jeremy dressed up as Clarke for a Halloween game, wearing a blond curly wig, blacked-out teeth, a No. 16 jersey with a captain's "C" on it, and a pair of Cooperall pants for warm-ups.

It was, as the great Bernie Parent might say, a beautiful thing.

J.R. was always loose, a funny guy who enjoyed himself and didn't take himself too seriously. Word got out that something was going to happen and that J.R. was behind it. He came out with the costume and it was hysterical. The fans loved it!

So did Clarkie. He was up in the press box watching warm-ups—and laughing so hard that he had to take off his glasses and wipe the tears from his eyes.

J.R. then went out and had a pair of assists and Brian Boucher made 27 saves as we beat the Penguins that night 3–0.

Halloween was always a fun night for me. Whenever we played that night—or near that night—I would put on my Groucho Marx glasses.

Wearing my Groucho Marx get-up, an annual passage, on Halloween in the 1980s.

It became a tradition for me. One year, I went to a dollar store and bought 10 Groucho disguises and took a bag with me for warm-ups and I laid them on the bench for all the off-ice officials—the penalty-box guys, the timer, and the penalty timekeeper. We all put them on at the same time and it got on ESPN.

Tom Coyle, who at that time worked the Flyers' penalty box, sat his disguise on the penalty bench. He didn't wear it the whole time. It was sitting there when Craig Berube, who was on the Flyers at the time, got a penalty and went to the box. I was following the game and listening on the headset and I heard, "Louie, Louie." I look over and it's Chief—Berube's nickname—and he has the nose and glasses on and this big-ass grin on his face. It was just hilarious. He didn't go on the ice with them. He had them on for 10 to 15 seconds and we laughed and then he took them off and was ready to go out on his shift.

Chief was one of the best guys who came into the penalty box—and he was there a lot. Just a great sense of humor.

Roger and His Ties

The late Roger Neilson, one of our former coaches, was a quirky guy and one of the all-time good people in the sport. He also happened to be...how can I say this politely? Let's just say he was not a slave to fashion.

Everybody always looked to see what kind of tie he'd wear. He wore some terrible, terrible ties. There's a pin out there that a lot of us have. It's a long tie that commemorates him and his taste. It's terrible, so it's perfect.

He had a tough time when he was with us, healthwise. When the team traveled, Joe Kadlec would take Roger for a drink or something to eat. One time he took Roger for a cancer treatment. Ed Snider told

Joe to stay with him and take care of him. Roger used to say, "When we travel, I'm Oscar Madison and Joe is Felix Unger. Joe is always meticulously dressed with every hair in place."

Roger was wonderful guy and always had time to talk. He'd ride his bike to practice, and physical conditioning was big part of who he was. He was just a wonderful, caring man and someone we all miss dearly.

When Roger was inducted into the Hockey Hall of Fame in 2002, he went shopping. Roger was anything but a clotheshorse, but he purchased a special tie for the occasion—a wild, gaudy bowtie that was in line with the ties that had become his trademark.

The tie was oh so fitting for him. His speech was also classic Roger.

"Doctors told me I should avoid excitement," he deadpanned to the audience in Toronto. "So I watch Leafs games."

The crowd roared, including Toronto coach Pat Quinn, who was sitting in Roger's sightline.

Roger was battling cancer at the time. That night, he called himself "the luckiest guy in the whole world" and noted he had been "just a Junior B goalie with limited skill" before getting a chance to coach Peterborough, one of the nation's top junior franchises.

"And then, 25 years, or whatever it is, in the NHL and had the chance to coach some of the greatest players in the game, and work with some of the top coaches and managers in the game," he said. "It's been a great ride."

Roger went on to call hockey the best of all the pro sports because of the skill and physical play that it involved. "And not only that, but it's got the best people," Roger said. "You talk to any hotel operator or bus driver or the airline people; they'll tell you every time that hockey guys are the best."

Roger certainly was.

CHAPTER 9
REMEMBERING ED SNIDER

When the 2016–17 season rolled around, there was a bitter-sweet feeling that engulfed the team and the Wells Fargo Center.

It was sweet because it was our 50th season in the NHL, and many special events were planned to celebrate the historic anniversary.

At the same time, it was bitter—and tinged with sadness—because the man most responsible for bringing the Flyers to Philadelphia, Ed Snider, wasn't there for the party.

On April 11, 2016, Ed died after a courageous two-year battle with bladder cancer.

It was strange and heartbreaking to look up to Suite 4 at the Wells Fargo Center and not see Ed in his familiar seat at our home games. People would often look up there after a pivotal play to see his reaction.

Before the 2016–17 season, Wayne Simmonds, our terrific right winger, said it best. He said it was unfortunate Ed wasn't around to celebrate the fruits of his labor, "but at the same time, he did leave a legacy. He left a great mark on the Philadelphia community and the NHL itself. So it'll be a celebration of the 50th year and Mr. Snider."

I was always proud that whenever I would introduce Ed to the fans, he would get cheers. When you think about it, the owners of sports teams don't often hear cheers. Ed always got them. These fans got what Ed was thinking about and what he did. The fans knew that, without him, none of this would have happened. Bob Clarke wouldn't have been an MVP; he may have done it with another team, but not here. The Stanley Cups wouldn't have happened here. The Russia game wouldn't have happened. None of it. *Poof!* It would all be gone and we'd be fans of other sports.

To me, that is the biggest thing I take from the legacy Ed has left. He made an indelible mark in my life. On all our lives, really.

I once told Ed that he has made an indelible mark on my life and he said, "You earned everything." I don't agree with that. I owe him an awful lot. He was just a great guy with tremendous foresight.

Ed was a very sentimental person. When they tore down the Spectrum in 2010, I was the emcee for the ceremony, and a lot of famous players who played in that building were there—Clarkie, Bernie Parent, Dr. J—and one by one they came up and said some things. Ed came up and talked. They had a big crane with a wrecking ball poised to knock down the building after all the dignitaries talked. Ed finished his speech and said, "Okay. I have to go. I'll see everybody later." He left. He couldn't be around to see the building demolished. I totally understand where he was coming from. The fight to build it, the fight to get teams in there, the fight to get the roof repaired when it blew off, the fight to getting the seats filled every night.

All those things had to be running around his mind. I'm sure he was thinking of all the good times there and all the people he worked with at the Spectrum—a Philadelphia institution—and it had to be tough. All the blood, sweat, and tears. All the late nights. All the promoting to get the Flyers off the ground in '67. He used to greet people as they walked through the turnstiles and try to get them to sign up for the Flyers' Fan Club. There were so many things that had happened to make that building work and make his team a success.

He walked off the stage during that 2010 ceremony and sped away in his SUV before the crane swung its huge concrete ball, which bounced off the building a couple times before it finally punched a hole through the bricks. It was as if the old girl did not want to go. And Ed didn't want to see the old girl go, either. He got in the car and his driver took off. Bingo. He was gone.

All of which brings to mind one of my favorites quotes from Ed: "Money should be the reward but not the reason."

A Hollow Feeling

It was difficult not having Ed here for our 50th anniversary. When I was at center ice for a ceremony, I looked up to his suite—it will always be *his* suite—and I felt like I saw him in his customary spot in the first row. And then I imagined that he was joining us from somewhere, taking great pride in the celebration.

It wasn't the same, but we battled through it because that's what Ed would have wanted. Keep it going.

It's amazing he was part of the Philadelphia sports scene for more than 50 years. Think about that. How many people can say that? He was an executive with the Eagles NFL team before he cofounded the Flyers with Jerry Wolman in 1966, one year before the franchise was on the ice for its first season.

When you look at all the Flyers team photos throughout the years, there was one constant: Ed. The players in the photos changed, but the guy in the center of the photo didn't.

Ed was the ultimate optimist when it came to his hockey team. He was one of the few who believed before the 2015–16 season that the Flyers would earn a playoff berth.

At the time, many brushed it aside as hyperbole from an out-of-touch owner.

But the Flyers, despite limitations, charged to the finish line and earned a playoff spot.

I know it may sound hokey and "win one for the Gipperish," but the Flyers used Ed's health battle as a rallying point. They visited him in his California mansion in late December that season and it left a lasting impression. When they arrived home from that road trip, they were a more focused team. They saw how much Ed was ailing and it pushed them to the limit.

Up to that point, they had just a 15–15–7 record. They went 26–12–7 the rest of way and secured a playoff spot, just as Ed had predicted.

Forward Brayden Schenn said it was difficult when the players visited Ed and "got to see what kind of shape he was in." He was an eye-opener for everyone. They knew he was failing. Schenn said that, in general, "guys are going to play hard" every night because of their pride. But seeing Ed made them play even harder. "He obviously cared about his players more than [most owners]," Schenn said. "The guys realized that and played hard for him."

It was so sad not to see Ed around the Wells Fargo Center for almost the entire 2015–16 season. He was such an animated presence when he was here, and he would go into the locker room after games and chat with the players and show them how much they meant to him. He was a one-of-a-kind owner.

Ed was a very positive thinker—not just with his hockey club, but with everything in his life. There were some not-so-good seasons during his 50 years, but he soldiered on and always looked at the bright side, always tried to make the team better.

At a service for Ed at the Wells Fargo Center, Bobby Clarke talked about how the Flyers were knocked out of a playoff spot when Buffalo's Gerry Meehan scored with four seconds left in the final regular-season game of the 1971–72 season.

Ed went into the locker room after the game, but instead of being furious, he consoled each of his players.

"He said, 'Boys, don't worry about it. We're going to be stronger for it,'" Clarke said. "Two years later, we won the Stanley Cup."

Don't get the wrong impression. There were many nights after a tough loss when you swore smoke was coming out of Ed's ears. You would see him flying down the hallway with a scowl—dressed in a suit and wearing his trademark orange tie—and you knew to get out of his way and not say anything. He wore his emotions on his sleeve. But he was always fair, always tough, always had his players' best interests in mind.

Ed used to get steamed when it was mentioned that there has been a long drought since we won our last Stanley Cup. He would talk about how it is much more difficult to win the Cup because there are 30 teams now, as opposed to 12 when we broke into the league.

Since the Flyers' inception in 1967, only Montreal and Boston have had a better winning percentage than Philadelphia. So even though we haven't won a Stanley Cup since 1975, we have been one of the NHL's best franchises.

Ed would turn red in the face when someone would bring up all the seasons without a Cup. He would always point to all the playoff appearances, all the top-notch seasons, all the times we reached the Finals.

"While we didn't win the other six times in the Stanley Cup Finals, we've reached the Finals three times in the 1980s, once in the 1990s, and in 2010," he once said. "I think it's a pretty damn good record, and one I'm very proud of."

Ed was a fan at heart. Not many owners in any sport get as emotionally involved with their teams as Ed did. He would call me from time to time on my phone in our ice-level box, wanting my feedback on some of the referee's calls that he thought weren't fair. You paid attention when Ed touched base with you. There was so much passion, so much fire in his voice. By the end of the conversation, I think he felt better—not because of what I said, but because he had a chance to blow off some steam.

Until the next "bad call" by one of the refs.

Leaving a Legacy

For all his success in hockey and business, Ed cared deeply about leaving this world a better place than when he entered it.

He always said one of his proudest accomplishments was the creation of the Ed Snider Youth Foundation, which provides youngsters from urban neighborhoods in Philadelphia and Camden with the opportunity to learn and play hockey.

Thousands of kids have played hockey thanks to the foundation, and the success has been astounding. It not only introduces the young players to hockey, but the kids must do work on their studies and they have done exceedingly well in the classroom. The youngsters who play know they must first take care of business in the classroom before they play hockey.

It helps them set goals at an early age and climb out of bad situations in their neighborhoods. One of the young women who spoke at Ed's memorial service at the Wells Fargo Center, Virlen Reyes, used to play hockey for the Ed Snider Youth Foundation. She later became captain of her college hockey team at West Chester University, leading it to the NCAA Division II national title. And she learned her hockey through the Ed Snider Youth Foundation.

At a ceremony celebrating Ed's life, Reyes, who was a 13-year-old from Kensington when she became involved with the foundation, said, "My future was as bleak as my environment. Crime was a big part of my five-day forecast, neighborhood drug deals were my basic studies in current events and economics, and the increase in dropout rates were my daily lesson in statistics."

Reyes joined the ESYHF, became the first from the foundation to go to college, and graduated with honors from West Chester University before being hired by Google Analytics.

"For the thousands of young people like myself who have been lucky enough to discover the Ed Snider Youth Foundation, we have a beautiful edge in life," Reyes said. "Through the foundation we have been taught to understand our own potential and to know that there is no limit in which we cannot reach. Mr. Snider's spirit will remain very much alive in each and every success story that comes from each and every participant of Snider Hockey."

Wow. What a beautiful testament to Ed and all the hardworking people who make his foundation a success.

Snider Hockey participants wrote letters and drew pictures to thank Snider, and they were displayed in the Wells Fargo Center concourse during his Celebration of Life ceremony.

Ed was once asked if the seeing the youth foundation grow was as rewarding as the consecutive Stanley Cups his Flyers won in 1974 and 1975.

"I can't compare," he said. "It would be like trying to compare your children. It's all good stuff."

The Ed Snider Youth Hockey Foundation was his legacy. The foundation, which started in 2005, partnered with the City of Philadelphia and the Commonwealth of Pennsylvania in 2010 to complete a $14.5 million construction project, completely refurbishing four public rinks for year-round use. The project included new classrooms, learning labs, and public meeting space.

The young players get ice time, uniforms, instruction, skates, and sticks for free. "Even before we took over the rinks, we did programs each year, and it's been a big thrill for me because for years we wanted to do something for inner-city kids," Snider once told the *Philadelphia Inquirer*. "I feel sad for what they have to go through in life.... The ice time helps them improve skills and keeps them off the street."

Ed was honored for his charity work by the Philadelphia Sports Writers Association in 2012, when the annual Ed Snider Lifetime Humanitarian Award was created. Ed could not have been more proud.

Tributes Pour In

During a heartfelt, 1-hour, 50-minute public memorial for Ed at the Wells Fargo Center, emotions poured out of people. The ceremony included speeches from three of his children, friends, business associates, NHL commissioner Gary Bettman, Philadelphia Mayor Kenney, and former Flyers great Bob Clarke.

Snider was remembered as a man of passion and wisdom.

"When I pass and when we all pass, we don't know where we're going," said a tearful Clarke, the Flyers captain when they won Stanley Cups in 1974 and 1975 and someone who has worked in several capacities with the team. "For me, I really hope when I get there, I get the chance to play one more game in the Orange and Black for Mr. Snider's Philadelphia Flyers."

Bettman was one of the many dignitaries who saluted Ed.

"He created a collection of achievements that belong in a museum," Bettman said. "And we're all part of that museum."

Bettman and Snider—the only owner to ever serve on the league's competition committee—became close. Bettman said Ed would sometimes end a conversation by telling him he loved him. "Which is not something a commissioner hears from his bosses," Bettman said.

Drew Katz, whose late father, Lewis, was Ed's best friend, said Snider was like a "second father" to him and that he could never repay him for the love and support he showed after his dad died in a plane crash.

Katz drew laughter from the crowd when he said Snider had once kicked Donald Trump out of the owner's suite "because he wouldn't stop talking to Ed during the game. No one came between him and his hockey games."

He said Ed was as tough as nails on the outside, "but soft as could be on the inside."

Brian Roberts, chairman and CEO of Comcast Corp., talked about how Ed started PRISM, which was a sports and entertainment network, and all-sports WIP radio. "Things that are taken for granted today all came out of his head. He was a genius," said Roberts, who called Snider a great listener who was "ferociously loyal" and the "perfect partner."

Roberts said Snider would visit his late father, Ralph, when his health was failing. "So this season, I had a chance to try to be there for Ed, at least a little bit."

About 30 seconds after every Flyers victory this season, Roberts said, he would phone Snider at his California home.

"No matter how sick or how much pain Ed was in," Roberts said, "he wanted and needed to talk about the Flyers. Ed lived for those wins. I lived for those calls."

At one point during his speech, Roberts was talking from the podium when his microphone temporarily blew out and made a loud noise that echoed around the arena.

"Hi, Ed," Roberts said, drawing laughs.

As he concluded his speech, Roberts went back to his days as a young Flyers fan.

"When I was a kid, every game ended—and Ed, I'm thinking of you now—with the great Gene Hart saying, 'Good night and good hockey.' And if I may add, 'Good life,'" Roberts said.

I couldn't have said it any better.

* * *

Several dozen former players attended the ceremony, including Clarke, the Flyers' senior vice president. Clarke asked the former players, and then the current players, to stand. He thanked the current players for winning their last playoff game against powerful Washington "for Mr. Snider."

The crowd gave both sets of players a rousing ovation.

The win over the Capitals enabled us to avoid elimination after losing the first three playoff games.

"To the Caps, if you're watching this: We're not done," said Jay Snider, Ed's son and the former Flyers president.

With heavy hearts, we then upset the Capitals in Washington 2–0 in Game 5 as Michal Neuvirth made 44 saves. That cut the Caps' series lead to three games to two. But our season ended with a hard-fought 1–0 loss in Game 6 at the Wells Fargo Center.

Lindy Snider, one of Snider's daughters, said the death of a parent leaves a "cold, empty place," but she told fans that "your tributes have warmed us."

The ceremony ended with Jacob Snider, Ed's grandson, singing a moving rendition of "What a Wonderful Life."

What a wonderful life, indeed.

Snider Estate Sells to Comcast

Someone recently posted the Flyers team photos on Facebook from over the years, and there was one constant: The proud guy sitting in the center, Ed.

Things are different without Ed. I'm not saying it's not good, but it's just not the same...and you wouldn't expect it to be. Ed *was* the Flyers. He was a one-of-a-kind guy and he is missed dearly. He was there for the team's birth, and was there for the ups and downs. Every single one of them.

It's sad he wasn't able to participate in all the festivities for the 50-year anniversary in 2016–17. He fought and fought and sure tried.

About five months after Ed's death, Comcast Corp. bought the portion of the Flyers and other Comcast Spectacor properties owned by his estate. That meant that for the first time since the Flyers were founded 50 years ago, the Ed Snider family was not part of the ownership group.

The estate had owned a 24 percent share. The year before Ed passed away, *Forbes* valued the Flyers at $660 million, seventh among the NHL's 30 teams.

With the deal, which was later approved by the NHL, cable giant Comcast owns 100 percent of the company, including the Flyers, four Skate Zone arenas, the Wells Fargo Center, and Spectra businesses.

But Ed's legacy will last forever. He cofounded the Flyers 50 years ago and introduced millions of people to what, at the time, seemed like a foreign sport.

"Ed was a visionary in the sports and entertainment industry and is deeply missed," said Roberts, chairman and CEO of Comcast Corp. "He planned for this transition and, thanks to his thoughtful approach on succession, Comcast Spectacor is in a strong position.

I'm very excited we are able to carry his spirit with us by bringing the company, its leadership, and its thousands of employees fully into the Comcast family."

Comcast Corp. officials said that the sale would not affect personnel. Comcast Spectacor president and CEO Dave Scott; Flyers president Paul Holmgren; Flyers general manager Ron Hextall; Wells Fargo Center president John Page; and Shawn Tilger, the Flyers' chief operating officer of business operations and senior vice president, remained in their same positions.

"We look forward to building on Ed's vision," Scott told the *Philadelphia Inquirer*.

Roberts said Scott was "handpicked three years ago" by Snider to direct Comcast Spectacor.

Scott is working closely with Holmgren and Hextall—as he has done since Snider became extremely ill a year ago—and is the person responsible for signing off on major decisions, such as signing a free agent.

"Dave will be the last word," Roberts said at the time. "My personal belief is you trust your leaders, you empower them, and they make the best decisions they can make."

Roberts added that Scott would "rely on the experts" in the Flyers' front office. "We're very confident this will work well. This is what Ed wanted. That's the most important message. He wanted us to own 100 percent, and he wanted a smooth transition."

The Snider family issued a statement, saying it was "delighted" that the team will be owned entirely by Comcast Corp. "While it is hard for us to imagine the Flyers without our father, Brian Roberts and Dave Scott recognize our passion for the team and consider our thinking. They continue to make us feel connected to the team," the family wrote. "Their respect enables us to feel a part of what our dad created and shared with millions of fans throughout Philadelphia."

According to Roberts, Snider had planned for Comcast Corp. to purchase his family's shares in the event of his death.

"Ed had put these wheels in motion years ago," Roberts said. "He wanted to provide for his family in other ways—and this does that for him."

Comcast Corp. purchased a majority of the Flyers in 1996. The agreement, called a "put and a call," stated that after the first year of the sale, Comcast Corp. could purchase—or Snider could sell—the rest of Snider's shares at any point, Roberts said.

When that 1996 deal was made, Comcast Spectacor assumed 66 percent of the Flyers, the 76ers, and the two arenas, after contributing $250 million in cash and stocks and assuming 66 percent of their combined $180 million debt, Roberts said at the time.

After Snider's death, one of his six children, Jay, said it would be "very emotionally difficult for my family, after 50 years, to be completely estranged and not to be involved [with the Flyers] in some way."

Roberts said the franchise would stay connected with the Sniders and "benefit from their wisdom and their passion for the Flyers."

Snider's children remain engaged in the Ed Snider Youth Hockey Foundation, preserving what their father wanted as his legacy. His daughter Lindy serves on the foundation's board of directors and executive committee.

Some of the money from the sale of the Snider estate was earmarked to support the youth foundation. That will help ensure that inner-city youth will have the opportunity to learn and play hockey.

Ed talked the talk and walked the walk.

After Ed's death, Scott was in constant contact with Snider's family members and said they would "continue to use Ed Snider's suite, Suite 4. It's been a smooth transition."

Shortly after the sale was announced, Scott had dinner with Jay Snider when he was in town. Scott wanted both sides to feel they were "still a part of where this all started."

Jay Snider, who was the Flyers president from 1983 to 1994, is busy running other businesses, including Airsoft Megastore, a Southern California online retailer that specializes in air guns for sport.

His dad was obviously the main person behind the Flyers, but he was involved in many other business ventures. Ed created Spectacor in 1974 as a management company to oversee the Flyers and the Spectrum. In the next 20 years, Spectacor grew, as did its impact on the sports and entertainment business. The company developed and acquired nearly a dozen related companies.

Some thought Ed ran the Flyers like a mom-and-pop operation because of the way he respected and rewarded his employees who showed loyalty. Many former Flyers have worked for the franchise throughout the years, long after their playing careers ended.

Roberts said the Flyers would not develop a big-business air just because they are owned exclusively by Comcast.

"I don't view this as a typical corporate structure," he told the *Inquirer*. "This is an entrepreneurial company that has thrived doing things like [rewarding former players].... We should not want to touch the fantastic structure. We want the Flyers to be the Flyers. A family."

At the time of his death, Ed was worth an estimated $2.5 billion, according to celebritynetworth.com. He amassed his wealth from humble beginnings—cutting meat, mopping floors, and performing other duties as a teenager at his father's grocery store in Washington, DC. No matter how menial the task, Ed took pride in what he did.

"He used to talk about how he cleaned the vegetable bins and how they were the cleanest vegetable bins ever," said Phil Weinberg, the longtime executive vice president and general counsel for Comcast Spectacor, the Flyers' parent company. "He learned a lot of his values and attention to detail from those everyday experiences of working for his father."

It was at his father's grocery store chain that Snider's entrepreneurial spirit was born. And grew. At the University of Maryland, he started a Christmas tree business with his fraternity brothers.

Not many people know about it, but Ed became a certified public accountant. But truth be told, he wanted to run the companies, not be the person keeping the books. In 1955, he and George Lilienfield started a wholesale record distributorship, Edge Ltd. They took out a loan and purchased about a half-million overstocked phonograph records at a deep discount.

"They were in boxes in a warehouse," Snider once said. "Recent records that just hadn't sold as expected."

After the deal, he loaded the records in the trunk of his car. Some were sold in his father's grocery stores; others were delivered to area grocery, discount, and drugstores. Three years later, he cofounded the National Association of Recording Merchandisers.

"I met him when he first came to Philly in '63," said Lou Scheinfeld, who was a reporter covering City Hall for the *Daily News* at the time and later was hired by Snider as the Flyers' first vice president.

Snider loved talking about his record-business days, Scheinfeld said.

"He was what they called a rack jobber. He and his partner took 45 RPM records and put racks in drugstores and other stores and filled the racks with them. They would go around every week or so and replace the ones that were sold and take back the ones that weren't sold."

They did well, Scheinfeld said, then got contracts for the PX stores at military bases in the Maryland/Virginia area.

"That contract helped them move a lot of records," he said. "But they realized they couldn't compete with the RCAs and the other big record companies, and they eventually sold their business."

Then Snider got a big break: a connection to Eagles owner Jerry Wolman. Snider's sister Phyllis—who years later suggested the name "Flyers" for the new hockey team—was married to Earl Foreman, Wolman's lawyer and part-owner of the Eagles. Wolman also had a strong friendship with Sol Snider, Ed's father.

Wolman asked Snider to run the Eagles' business side, Scheinfeld said.

"Ed said, 'What do I know about running a football team?'" Scheinfeld recalled. "He said, 'Well, you don't, but you're smart and you know money.' So that's how Ed came to Philly."

In 1964, Ed became treasurer and vice president of the Eagles. In 1966, he and Wolman helped bring an NHL expansion team to Philadelphia, though the Flyers didn't begin playing until the 1967–68 season.

Ed was just getting started. In 1973, he created Spectacor as a management company to oversee the Flyers and the Spectrum. The move helped launch an entire industry: private management of sports and entertainment facilities typically run by the cities, universities, or stadium authorities that owned them.

In the next 20 years, Spectacor grew, as did its impact on the sports and entertainment business, developing and acquiring nearly a dozen related companies.

The man was a genius in the business world.

Ed merged Spectacor with Comcast Corp. in 1996, forming Comcast Spectacor, which initially consisted of the Flyers, the 76ers, the American Hockey League Phantoms, the CoreStates Center (now the Wells Fargo Center), and the Spectrum. The company later joined with the Phillies to form Comcast SportsNet regional cable networks.

Dave Scott, Comcast Spectacor's president and CEO, called Ed a risk taker and a "forward-thinking guy" who will "always be the heart and soul of our company."

Holmgren worked closely with Snider, first as the Flyers' general manager, then in his current position as club president.

Snider had an intuitive sense for what needed to be done.

"One of the great things about Ed was he could size up a situation in a flash and make a decision," Scheinfeld said. "I mean, bing-bing-bing, done. That carried him throughout his entire career."

"His big saying was that he hired people to do a job and he let them do the job with the resources he gave them," said Holmgren, who was a forward for the Flyers from 1976 to 1984. "He trusted the people he put in place."

On player-personnel decisions, Holmgren said, Ed was "famous for never saying no to you, really. He would challenge you, he would argue with you to the bitter end if you wanted to make a trade or sign a player, or even redesign the dressing room. But then he would say, 'If you think that's for the best, it's fine.' He was very supportive once you made a decision on what you wanted to do."

When the sale of the team was announced, Scott said the 20-year mortgage on the Wells Fargo Center was recently paid off and that Comcast Spectacor "has never been in better financial shape than it is right now.... And when you put all that together, it's allowed the focus to be, 'Let's try to win the Stanley Cup in Ed's memory and make him proud.'"

Sounds like a good plan, Dave.

CHAPTER 10

THE REAL BROAD STREET BULLIES

When people around the country think of the Flyers, the nickname "Broad Street Bullies" probably pops into their mind. That colorful nickname, coined by sportswriter Jack Chevalier of the old *Evening Bulletin*, was more fitting in the days when fighting was a major part of the game.

The game has evolved into a fast-paced style and, because of the rule changes, fighting is far less prevalent today.

I love today's game, love the speed and the artistry. But, to be honest, a big part of me misses the old-time hockey style that produced so many great characters who are permanently etched in our minds.

On November 17, 2016, as part of the Flyers' 50th anniversary year, the franchise honored some of the tough guys in our history. There were many of them, and they changed the fortunes of countless games in Orange and Black history.

Don't get the wrong idea. The Flyers didn't "goon" their way to wins during their glory days. That's a misnomer. You see, there was tons of talent on their best teams, led by Bernie Parent, Bobby Clarke, Rick MacLeish, Bill Barber, Gary Dornhoefer, Reggie Leach, Jimmy Watson, among many others.

A plethora of gifted forwards, an underrated defense, and the best goalie on the planet led us to Stanley Cup championships in 1974 and 1975. Toughness supplemented that talent. Was it an important part of the team? No question. But it wasn't the main reason for our success.

With that in mind, here are here are my 10 toughest Flyers of all time.

1. Dave Schultz

They called him the Hammer, and for good reason. He may have lost a fight during his four seasons with the Flyers, but I can't remember one.

Schultzy was Clarke's unofficial bodyguard. If you took a cheap shot at Clarkie—and many teams did before Schultz arrived—you paid a price. Even without Schultz, Clarke played with a fearlessness that was hard to match. With Schultz, he became even more fearless—if that was possible.

Dave watched out for all his teammates during those great years when we won our Cups. He knew his role very, very well, and he also was a better player than people remember. He scored 20 goals in the season that we won our first Cup (1973–74), and had some big playoff goals for us, including the overtime winner in Atlanta to win the first-round series in 1974.

Yes, he made his mark with his fists and with his intimidation, but he was also a pretty good player in his own right.

I'll never forget how he would get when he got into a fight. He got big eyes and they would bulge out. He was sort of out of control, and the refs would have a difficult time settling him down and getting him to go to the penalty box.

The fight I remember the most is the one with Dale Rolfe. Game 7 of the 1974 Stanley Cup semifinals at the Spectrum. That was back when hair-pulling wasn't against the rules. He grabbed Rolfe by the back of the head and started firing punches. By one count, he outpunched Rolfe 17–2. No Rangers came to help Rolfe. Nobody. The Rangers just watched and I think that fight spelled the end of the Rangers. That wouldn't have happened with our guys. Our guys had each other's backs.

When the fight took place, the game was scoreless, but it seemed to spark us, seemed to put us back on track. We ended up winning 4–3 and going to the Finals and winning our first Cup by beating the Boston Bruins in six games.

I often wonder what would have happened if Schultz hadn't fought Rolfe and taken the energy out of the Rangers. Maybe they would have won the game and *they* went on to win the Cup.

Schultzy was all business even when he came into the penalty box. Some of the guys would say, "Hey, Lou, how are things?" or make some kind of small talk. He wasn't like that. After a fight he was just so riled up that you couldn't even talk to him. It took him a while to calm down—probably the entire five minutes of the penalty—before he had come back to his senses.

Ed Snider loved Schultz. In Blake Allen's book *Keith the Thief* about his dad, Keith, our general manager at the time, Ed's devotion to Schultzy was spelled out.

In his foreword, Snider wrote that a few years after the Flyers traded Schultz, he was "pushing and pushing to bring Davey back until finally Keith erupted.

"You want him so goddamn badly, I'll get him for you," Allen said, according to Snider.

Added Snider: "To me, that said, 'You're the owner, but this is against my better judgment."

Snider backed down. Schultz wasn't brought back.

It's also my understanding that Ed had a lot to do with Schultz going into the Flyers Hall of Fame. He wasn't one of the best players in franchise history, but he was one of the most important ones because of the way he could change a game. He was integral to our team winning the two Cups.

2. Behn Wilson

Behn was one of the best fighters we have ever had. When he was younger, he came up and had a few fights, and once word got around about how tough he was, *nobody* wanted to fight him. He had a short career here, but he left a lasting impression.

He had a different fighting style than Schultzy, who might take a punch just so he could get a hold of your jersey—and then become the aggressor. But Behn would go at it right away. He was a wild man. It was, "Come on. Let's go." No finesse. No clutching or grabbing and trying to hold on to his opponent. He just dropped the gloves and went at it. He wouldn't take a punch before delivering his own.

Wilson was also an offensive defenseman who reached double figures in goals in six seasons, including 16 tallies for the Flyers in 1980–81.

3. Donald Brashear

At 6'3", 237 pounds, Brashear was a physical specimen, one of the strongest players I have ever seen. After we acquired him from Vancouver in 2001, he looked out for all his teammates. He could really fight, and he was so strong that when he hit you, he could make you stagger. He left a lot of opponents dazed and woozy.

One thing I remember about him is that young tough guys wanted to fight him because they knew if they could hang in there with Brash, it would help their reputation. And when he gave them a fight and they would come back to the penalty box, the young guys would thank him for the opportunity.

Brash was a nice guy. A pleasant man. A lot of guys who were intense on the ice—Brash, Schultzy, Ron Hextall, Paul Holmgren, Dave Brown, just to name a few—were quiet and soft-spoken off the ice. It's funny how that happens. On the ice, it's like a switch is thrown.

4. Mel Bridgman

Mel was one of our toughest guys ever. He was captain here for a while, and he was a great leader. It's hard to remember him ever losing a fight. He may have had a draw somewhere, but he won almost every scrap he was in. He had a great center of gravity because he was a pretty good skater, and that made it almost impossible to knock him down—as opposed to Homer (Holmgren), who fell down a lot. Mel could throw them. Just a very solid guy.

We gave up a lot to get Mel, whom we selected with the first overall pick in the 1975 draft.

On June 4, 1975, we traded center Bill Clement, who scored a critical insurance goal when we won our second Cup the previous month, minor-league defenseman Don McLean and our first-round pick (18th overall) to Washington to acquire him. Freddy Shero said the price was worth it. Bridgman was his type of player, a guy who wasn't afraid to go into the corner to get the puck—even though he knew he would absorb a punishing hit to come out with it.

In juniors, Mel was a sensational scorer, but he arrived in Philadelphia on a great team and had to change his role, going from a top-line forward to a checking-line center who killed penalties and played against opponent's top lines. He was a solid two-way player.

Give him credit for making a smooth and unselfish transition.

5. Dave Brown

Brownie was tall, with long arms and good range, and that made him a great fighter. He didn't have to get you from inside, because he could get you from outside with his long reach. So if you had a smaller reach, you were in big trouble. He played in the era when the jerseys could come off; they didn't have the tie-down like they have now. So when he had longer fights, he made sure the jersey would go. Today, the jerseys are tied to the pants, and if the jersey comes off, you get a penalty.

I'll never forget Brownie coming out of the locker room in that pregame fight in Montreal in 1987. This was before Game 6 of the Prince of Wales Conference final at the hallowed Forum. Again, this was during warm-ups, so there were no referees to break up the ruckus.

Dave came roaring out of the locker room in his hockey underwear and went at it with a couple guys. Claude Lemieux had shot a puck into our empty net at the end of warm-ups, and all hell broke loose. Most of the guys had already left the ice and had gone into the locker room. Doug Crossman came back on without skates. Pat Croce was the trainer and he was trying to hold back Crossman from the fight. There was one fight after another after another. Brownie and Montreal's Chris Nilan were among the combatants, and the organist was playing some dentist-office music while chaos reigned on the ice.

Ed "Boxcar" Hospodar and Chico Resch had gone toward our locker room, but they raced back onto the ice when they saw what Lemieux did.

"Chico was an innocent bystander; a nice reborn Christian guy, and I took him to the dark side," Hospodar told the *Globe and Mail.*

The brawl caused the NHL to introduce tougher legislation, increase suspensions, and add stiff fines. Bench-clearing brawls gradually disappeared.

Before the Montreal fiasco, the league "didn't do anything to stop the brawling," Hospodar said. "I was a knucklehead. I was getting a big fat check. You want to fix something, hit the players in their wallet. That gets their attention every time."

6. Rick Tocchet

Rick was a tough guy who could do it all. He could fight and he could score a ton of goals—in a way, he was similar to Wayne Simmonds nowadays. Rick really meant a lot to this team. Toc would throw off the gloves and go at it. There was no hesitation.

Toc developed into a great power forward—he scored 440 goals in his career, including 232 in 621 games with the Flyers—and as he gained experience, he became more controlled in knowing when to drop the gloves and when to skate away.

7. Paul Holmgren

Homer was another guy who could fight and play with skill. He had pretty good hands, and he scored 138 goals in 500 games with us. He was a big, hulking farmer-type player from Minnesota who was another guy who had a lot of fights. It seemed like he had a lot of them with Willi Plett when he was with the Flames. They were knock-down, drag-'em-out jobs.

And who can forget his monumental battle with Boston's Wayne Cashman at the Spectrum in 1977? In a preseason game, no less.

Cashman and Jimmy Watson were ejected for getting into a stick duel, and Holmgren was then booted for being the third man into the altercation. Homer and Cashman continued to jaw at each other as they left the ice and they fought each other in the short hallway separating the two dressing rooms. Before you knew it, several players were underneath the stands throwing punches. There were 16 game misconducts handed out. That left just eight Bruins and nine Flyers left to play in the exhibition game.

Afterward, workers installed an iron gate between the home and visiting locker rooms at the Spectrum, making it much more difficult for a brawl to occur after players left the ice.

Back in those days, players would look to start a fight because their team needed a spark, and there was usually someone on the other team who would be there to fight you. Nowadays, players turn around and they don't want to go at it. For the most part, that's out of the game now. Not many teams carry enforcers anymore.

Back then, a team would be down, say, 4–1, and they needed a wake-up call, so someone would drop the gloves. His teammates and management appreciated it. It was part of the code, part of what made the NHL so popular.

Now the emphasis is on speed and skill. It's still an exciting game, a great game. But, to be honest, part of me misses the old days. I'm a hockey purist. I always liked the game because it was rough. That element has gone out of the game since Gary Bettman came along as the commissioner. The owners love Bettman and he's brought them into a different era. But I'm not so sure I share that love for the way the game has changed.

I look through the box scores every day to see who's fighting, and not many of them are. It's a different time.

8. Eric Lindros

When Eric first came into the league, he gained his skating room. Guys would hang all over him and he would just turn around and drop the gloves and beat the crap out of them. And he could. Big hands. Long arms. Hulk of a guy. And he would just clobber people.

And then I kind of think he had a talking to and was told he was more valuable on the ice than serving a five-minute major. I agree with that, but I also think when he didn't fight much anymore, that changed the way people looked at him and that was the beginning of when the concussions started. Guys started to run at him a little bit and that was the beginning of a series of concussions.

Eric was the quintessential power forward. In today's game, he might even be better than he was in his day—and he was a Hall of Famer—because guys would fear suspensions and wouldn't take as many runs at him.

9. Glen Cochrane

He was a guy who had your back all the time, and he wasn't afraid to take a punch to give a punch. I have him ranked above several other good fighters because he had no fear of anyone. He had pretty good size, and he would fight anybody. Back in those days, every team had one or two guys who were real good fighters, and Glen was challenged by people who could hold their own. Nowadays, it's hard to pick out just who is the so-called tough guy on a lot of teams.

For a couple years, Cochrane was paired with Mark Howe, who would become a Hall of Famer. Glen saved Howe some wear and tear and made sure no one took a run at him. The pair combined for a plus-89 rating—Howe was at plus-47, Cochrane at plus-42—in 1982–83. Cochrane also had 237 penalty minutes that season.

10. Bob Kelly

I originally had Ron Hextall here, but after a lot of deliberation, I went with the Hound.

Shero would pick the opportune time and turn Kelly loose. Say we were down a goal or two, he'd send the Hound over the boards and he was like a wild pinball—shooting here, shooting there. Bouncing off people and causing havoc that invariably got us going. *Bang, bang, bang*. All good hits and he would change the game because it got the crowd into it even more.

And when the Hound got into a fight, it seemed like he set a record for the amount of punches thrown. He was tireless, and he would wear down the guy he was fighting.

The Hound was tenacious in the corners, a relentless checker and someone who was called the Pete Rose of hockey because of his all-out hustle. For good measure, he kept things loose in our colorful dressing room. Schultzy once called him "our lead clown" because he always had an amusing one-liner to keep the boys smiling.

As for Hexy, it's hard to forget his epic fight against Felix Potvin—he skated down the other end of the ice to go after him—and the way he stood up for his teammate and went after Montreal defenseman Chris Chelios. Hexy was just so competitive and hated to lose.

During Game 6 of the 1989 Eastern Conference finals, Hexy went after Chelios because he had knocked Brian Propp unconscious with an elbow to the head in the first game of the series.

In that series' final game, Hextall got some revenge.

"Did you see what he did to Brian Propp?" he said at the time. "C'mon. I think we owed him something. God Almighty, he just about took his head off. I think that's good enough reason" to retaliate.

Others Who Deserve Mention

Bobby Clarke was the meanest hockey player I ever saw—and I mean that as a compliment. He would almost kill you to win. Losing wasn't an option. He could get you going with a great pass or goal, or he could send a message to his team by going out of his way to agitate an opponent with a well-placed stick or glove. Talk about tough guys. Clarkie would be bleeding all over the place and he didn't even care. It was just part of his shift, part of who he was.

His teammates had his back, too. There was a 1973 game against the California Golden Seals at the Spectrum, and Barry Cummins, retaliating after taking a stick to the face, sent Clarkie down in blood, and *bam*, the entire benched emptied and went after Cummins. Cummins, who was playing in his first and, as it turned out, his only NHL season, left the ice more bruised than anybody.

We were leading 2–1 in the second period when Cummins hit Clarke over his head with a two-handed swing of his stick, opening a gash that would take 20 stitches to close.

The Flyers, led by Bill "Cowboy" Flett, went after Cummins en masse, and the rookie defenseman left the ice bloodied. Later in the period, there was another long, bench-clearing brawl.

Clarkie returned in the third period, and after the Flyers' 5–1 win ended, he received an apologetic phone call from Cummins.

In *Full Spectrum*, Cummins said it was an "impulse" reaction to getting cut below the eye by Clarke—he later received three stitches—and that "he regretted it as soon as it happened."

The Flyers' togetherness was never more evident than how they rushed to aid Clarke. He was the guy who was going to lead them to the promised land, they realized. The message: You mess with our leader, you are going to pay the price.

Clarkie was the heart and soul of our hockey teams. He didn't have the natural skating skills of a Bobby Orr or a Guy Lafleur or a Steven Stamkos, but he played with a fervor that was unmatched. Coupled with his great talent to find the net, he became one of the greatest players in NHL history.

Because he was a diabetic, he wasn't picked until 17th overall in the 1969 amateur draft. I think that made him more determined to show NHL teams they had made a mistake by passing on him.

He spent 14 seasons proving them wrong.

Hail, Lappy

Ian Laperriere is another former Flyer who deserves special mention.

I am not overstating things when saying that the player known as "Lappy" was a warrior. Now a Flyers assistant coach, he did everything to win a game when he played, no matter the price. Whether it was throwing his body in front of an opponent's slap shot, checking someone into the boards, or dropping his gloves against a much bigger player, Lappy was a true Flyer, a relentless fourth-line grinder who helped us get to the Stanley Cup Finals in 2010.

There was a T-shirt featuring his battered image that became a popular item. The words on the T-shirt said it all: PUT ON YOUR LAPPY FACE.

Early in the 2009–10 season, Ian lost seven teeth and required 100 stitches after taking a slap shot in the face against Buffalo.

Naturally, he returned to the lineup in the third period of that game.

In the opening round of the playoffs that season, Lappy's vision was blurred and his brain was bruised when he absorbed a shot taken by New Jersey's Paul Martin. Blood gushed from above his right eye. Laperriere received about 70 stitches, and a CAT scan revealed a spot on his brain.

Doctors said he would likely miss the rest of the playoffs.

Instead, Laperriere returned to the lineup a month later, facing the Montreal Canadiens in the Eastern Conference finals.

"The day I stop doing that," he said of his fearless shot blocking, "I'll retire."

Post-concussion symptoms caused him to miss the 2010–11 and 2011–12 seasons. But he had one more moment in the spotlight. In 2011, Lappy was honored with the Bill Masterton Memorial Trophy, awarded to the NHL player who best exemplifies the qualities of perseverance, dedication to the game, and sportsmanship.

In June 2012, Lappy was finally forced to retire at age 38. He was asked how he wanted to be remembered.

"Just to be remembered would be nice," he said with a smile. "It's the name of the game—the new flavors coming in the next year. It's fine, but at the same time, you miss that and it's kind of hard to swallow, I guess. But at the end of the day I'm lucky because I played close to 1,100 games and I was hoping as a little boy to play one game. I surpassed that and I played a lot longer than I ever expected."

Known for his quick wit and friendly demeanor, Laperriere was an expert penalty killer who played in 1,083 regular-season games and 67 playoff contests, including all six with the Flyers in the 2010 Cup Finals against Chicago. During his career, he registered 121 goals, 336 points, and God knows how many stitches.

"The way I played the game was fighting and being physical, and I was looking around and it's tough to find guys that play my way who played that long," he said. "It's a matter of when you're going to get a career-ending injury—it's not a matter of if, it's a matter of when. I feel very fortunate and very proud of what I did."

When you look up the word *inspiring* in the dictionary, there isn't a picture of Ian Laperriere next to the word.

But there should be.

Nolet a Tough Guy?

Simon Nolet had great hands and knew how to put the puck in the net. Scoring was his calling card, but he could fight when it was needed.

John Ferguson was one of the toughest guys in the NHL, but Simon pounded him in a game in Montreal. It was amazing because not many people think of Simon as a fighter.

Rick MacLeish and Mark Recchi were others who were known for their scoring, but they could throw punches with the best of them. There was a game in which MacLeish sent Detroit's Henry Boucha to the ice with a punch that the center never saw coming.

Most of the fighters are the nicest people you'd ever want to meet. Take Jody Shelley and Jay Rosehill, two forwards who played for us. They were our last true enforcers, and they were always quick with a quip when they came to the penalty box. They didn't take themselves too seriously and they had lots of fun on the ice and in the locker room. They were two guys who were truly team leaders.

Some of our fighters had distinctive styles. Take Jack McIlhargey and Kelly. They would throw rapid-fire punches—*boom-boom-boom-boom-boom*—barely after the gloves were dropped. Bucky (McIlhargey) was a little bit crazy. And the Fridge (Todd Fedoruk) was a massive guy who did great things until he took a punch to the face.

Former Flyer Simon Nolet chats with me at the Spectrum during the 1974–75 season. Nolet returned to Philly with the Kansas City Scouts.

I also have a special place in my heart for Andre Dupont. The Moose was such a tough player and he had a mean streak in him that, for the most part, was used at the right time. Moose was Moose. He didn't drop his gloves very often, but when he did, he left an imprint.

Epilogue

I remember when Swedish players came into the league, our guys would go after them because they had the reputation of not being tough. Now, Finnish guys were different. The Finns were tougher. I'll probably hear from the Swedish guys, but they weren't fighters. Russians didn't fight much either. I don't think they were allowed.

Our identity evolved into a hardnosed team after we got pushed around by the Blues in the early years. Guys like Noel Picard and the Plager brothers abused us, and Ed Snider said it would never happen again. That started a trend for drafting guys who were comfortable playing a bruising style; guys like Schultz, Kelly and Don Saleski.

We were a small team—a bunch of guys who looked like accountants—in our first couple years. But we got bigger and feistier after that. We kind of reflected our general manager back then, Keith Allen.

Keith was also our first coach, and he was the perfect man to start the franchise. Bud Poile was our first general manager, and he was familiar with Keith when he hired him. Bud was a player-coach in Detroit's minor-league system and Keith was a defenseman for him.

Quite fittingly, Keith's first team was defensively sound. We had two good goalies—Bernie Parent and Doug Favell—and a very responsible defensive team, one that included Joe Watson and Ed Van Impe.

We were a hard team to play against, and that kind of became our calling card for a lot of years. In our first year, we beat each of the Original Six teams at least once, and a lot of credit for that season belongs to Keith and the system he implemented.

As I mentioned earlier, the game has changed dramatically from when we first came into the league. Back then, the players used to police themselves.

In today's game, fines and suspensions make players think twice about standing up for a teammate. You get suspended for, say, five games, it's going to cost you a huge chunk of money. You start racking up game misconducts, it hits you in the wallet. And the money they lose isn't chicken feed anymore.

Personally, I think the NHL has gotten too soft. I do, however, understand that the ongoing health of the players is what's important. It's a legal issue, too. Some players are suing the league because of concussions they sustained when playing and their health issues later in life. All I'm saying is, we can say we long for old-time hockey, but the truth of the matter is that the health of these players is paramount to anything else.

It wouldn't be surprising if down the road, fighting is totally outlawed. You can see it coming. Back in the day, fighting was an outlet. Guys like Schultz made their living that way. Schultz wasn't a bad player, but he made the league because of his toughness. A lot of guys were like that. Some guys were in the league because their physical play enabled the superstars to have room on the ice.

It's strange when you compare eras. In the old days, when players didn't have helmets and shields, you didn't see many high sticks. Now, sticks are higher because they know their opponent is protected by equipment. Does that mean we have too much equipment? No. But has it had an effect on the way the game is played? No question.

CHAPTER 11
ONE LAST REUNION

In mid-January of 2017, the Flyers held a reunion weekend to celebrate their 50th anniversary. It was, by all accounts, a wild success.

It was a wonderful two days. They were days all of us cherished, because we know it was the last time one of these big-time reunions will ever be held. I don't know how something like it can ever be equaled. It brought together players from every Flyers decade, including the start of the franchise in 1967.

Hey, if there's a 100-year reunion and the Flyers are still around, I'll be pushing up daisies somewhere, as will most of the people who were at this weekend celebration.

On a Friday, at the Sugar House Casino in Philadelphia, we had a meet-and-greet with fans and a reception. The next day there was an alumni game against the Pittsburgh Penguins at the Wells Fargo Center.

For two days, everybody associated with the Flyers and Penguins walked around with perpetual grins. From beginning to end, it was a huge smilefest. People hugging one other because they hadn't seen each other for a long time, and story after story after story.

The camaraderie was tremendous. As for our reunion, it was a spectacular. Guys came in from all over, and the Flyers really did things first-class.

It was especially good to see the guys who were original Flyers from our first season in 1967–68. Joe Watson and Bernie Parent were two of them, but they still work for the organization so I get to see their friendly faces all the time. But it was also great to see other original Flyers, including Lou Angotti, John Miszuk, Don Blackburn, Brit Selby, Garry Peters, Forbes Kennedy, and Doug Favell.

Some of those guys I hadn't seen in decades, and it was refreshing to see them. We all picked up right where we left off, whether it was in the 1960s, 1980s, or whenever. The one thing that permeated the entire weekend was happiness. There were hundreds of photos taken, and you didn't have to ask anyone to smile because they all had permanent grins on their faces. Some of the older guys hadn't had this kind of adulation in years, and they really ate it up and enjoyed themselves.

As for the alumni game, I got to announce the rosters from both teams. I went out to center ice, the spotlight came on and I did a recap of our 50-year history. The lights went down and they played a video of guys scoring big goals and beating people up, and a lot of the key plays from the last five decades. It was tough to boil down 50 years into a relatively short presentation, but they did a wonderful job. We also paid tribute to all the people connected to the organization who we have lost over the years and it was very compelling.

I introduced all the players on both sides, one by one, and the biggest ovation went to Clarkie. But *everybody* got huge ovations, especially Bernie Parent, Eric Lindros, Johnny LeClair, Simon Gagne, and Danny Briere.

When Lauren Hart came out to sing the "God Bless America" duet on the split screen with the video of Kate Smith, it was an emotional moment. Lauren had tears rolling down her face and she did a great job. And then the puck dropped and it was fun, fun, fun.

The game drew a sellout crowd, and that tells everything you need to know about the love affair between the Flyers and the fans.

Despite not winning a Stanley Cup since 1975, the fans have remained incredibly loyal throughout the 50 years.

Never was that more evident than when the fans packed the Wells Fargo Center for the alumni game against the Penguins, a matchup between two of the six expansion teams that entered the NHL in 1967.

The teams played to a 3–3 tie (nothing wrong with ties!) before an appreciative crowd. I thought it would be a wild 8–7 or 9–8 game, but the goalies stood tall. Neil Little and Brian Boucher were in the nets for us—Boosh even stopped a penalty shot—and we got goals from Danny Briere, Dave Brown, and Eric Desjardins. Terry Crisp, who played on our two Stanley Cup championship teams and later coached Calgary to a Cup, served as our coach that night, and Crispy was chirping like crazy behind the bench. As usual. Moose Dupont and Dave Schultz assisted him in changing the lines and the defense, and there was a lot of good-natured ribbing going on. Everybody was busting on one another and enjoying themselves.

Some fans wanted the game to go into overtime, but I think most of them were just happy to have one more night with the greatest players in franchise history.

And besides, some of the players looked like they were going to pass out! They were gassed from playing their first game in a long, long time. Bobby Clarke enjoyed himself immensely, but he said it was the last alumni game he would ever play in. "It's time to pass the torch to some of the younger alumni," he said. Bill Barber said the same thing. So the 19,000-plus who attended the game could say they saw the end of an era—and I know some of those fans were probably at the first games that Clarke and Barber ever played, back in the old Spectrum.

"When you're playing and you know it's your last game, you appreciate it," said Clarke, who holds numerous Flyers records. "In front of a crowd like this, it's special. To get a reception like this game..."

Clarkie searched for the right words.

"Only in Philadelphia," he said.

Clarkie made a poignant comment to reporters after the game, which was held about nine months after the beloved Ed Snider had passed away.

"We were awfully close," he said of Snider. "And he hasn't deserted me at all yet. I still think of him often."

* * *

The game featured players from every Flyers decade, including the famed "LCB" and "Legion of Doom" lines. Reggie Leach, Clarke and Barber formed the former line, while LeClair, Lindros, and Mikael Renberg formed the latter.

Representation ranged from Watson, a defenseman who was an original Flyer on the 1967–68 team, to Briere and Gagne, forwards on the team that reached the Stanley Cup Finals in 2010.

In honor of their 50-year anniversary, the Flyers also brought back many of their former stars for pregame festivities during the 2016–17 season to relive memorable moments.

But while the focus was on the many heroes who have worn the Orange and Black, there was another group that deserved serious mention.

"The fans," Lindros said, "were always incredible in Philly."

I second that feeling.

Oh, the fans may boo on occasion in an attempt to wake up players, but they have filled virtually every seat for the longest of times.

At the alumni game, the players, to a man, were astonished by the sellout. I did six or seven interviews for TV that night, and almost all the players talked about how amazed they were by the crowd.

Lindros, who was inducted into the Hockey Hall of Fame in November, never took the fans for granted. When he played, he wanted to reward them for their loyalty. For proof, go to YouTube and watch Lindros, his voice cracking, his eyes filled with tears, in his emotional speech when he accepted the 1994–95 Hart Trophy as the league's MVP.

"In closing," he said toward the end of his speech, "I'd just like to say, thank you to the Philadelphia fans who supported us when we weren't so good."

And here, Eric became choked up with tears. After a long pause, he composed himself, barely, and said: "We're getting better and we're going to do it."

The Flyers never won a Cup during the Lindros era. Fact is, they haven't won one in 42 years. But the fans keep filling the arena,

When Lindros and LeClair were inducted into the Flyers Hall of Fame in 2014, both said the fans pushed their careers to a higher level.

"You guys are awesome," LeClair told the standing fans before separate banners with his name and his former linemate's were raised to the rafters. "You didn't accept losing."

LeClair thanked the fans for "the continuous energy" they gave him.

Lindros had a similar theme.

"Night in and night out, you brought passion to the Wells Fargo Center," he said. "We felt you and played for you."

At the November Hall of Fame ceremony in Toronto, Lindros said, "Philly fans are terrific. They really are. There aren't many cities in the States where you get that feeling. You get it here in Toronto, obviously, and in every Canadian city. I think Philly is top-notch in terms of the US side of things."

Announcing ceremonies in which Eric Lindros and John LeClair were inducted into the Flyers Hall of Fame in 2014.

A Sellout for "Has-Beens"

After the alumni game in January, the participants seemed awestruck by the crowd.

"A sellout to watch a bunch of us has-beens," goalie Brian Boucher said with a smile. "Can't say enough about the fans."

"I wouldn't have changed anything. I would have played with one leg, to be honest with you," Hall of Fame left winger Bill Barber said. "To have the opportunity to be out there for our fans, we have the greatest fans in the world and I thank them for that. It was a real pleasure to play here in Philly in front of a crowd like that."

Briere agreed.

"It's all you need to know about Flyers fans," he said. "To get 20,000 people to come out for guys that are past their prime. That's all you need to know. It's just simply amazing."

Briere said it was great for him and the other players "to have one more day to live our dream. I still have goose bumps just thinking about it. To get on the ice for the warm-up and to see the whole building already full...to play with legends. It was a blast."

Carl Luzi, 61, who owns an insurance and retirement planning agency in West Berlin, New Jersey, attended the alumni game with his 26-year-old son, C.J.

The elder Luzi spoke for most of the fans when he called the game "a real tribute to the organization, including Ed Snider."

Snider, of course, was one of the team's cofounders, and he was the Flyers' chairman until his death in the spring of 2016.

"I think the roof would have blown off if 88's shot had hit the back of the net to win it late in the game," Luzi added, referring to Lindros. "All in all, it was a life moment for all of us in the Flyers family."

Eric and LeClair had grade-A chances at the end of the game, but they were turned aside by Penguins goalie Jocelyn Thibault. Nobody likes ties, but I think everyone went home satisfied—and thrilled—that they got a chance to watch 50 year's worth of their heroes that night.

The loudest cheers may have come when Snider was shown on the scoreboard in a series of photos, a tribute to the man who had the foresight to believe hockey could make it in Philadelphia. Turned out he was right.

"You'll Be in Baltimore in Six Months!"

When you hear all the glowing tributes to the fans, it's easy to forget that Philly wasn't always a hockey hotbed.

Snider took a huge risk when he cofounded the team. At the time, Philadelphia did not have a good track record of supporting major- or minor-league hockey teams.

In 1967, after returning from Quebec City and their first training camp, the Flyers tried to drum up fan interest by holding a parade down Broad Street.

About two-dozen people showed up.

"There were more people *in* the parade than there were people watching it," said Watson, a onetime Flyer who is now a senior account executive for the Wells Fargo Center's advertising department. "I said, 'Hell, we're not going to be here very long.' One fan gave me the finger and said, 'You'll be in Baltimore in six months!'"

The franchise was purchased for $2 million, and Snider and Jerry Wolman got the Spectrum built for $12 million. A bogus contest was held to name the team. The winner was "Flyers," but Snider's sister, Phyllis, had actually chosen that name months earlier.

General manager Bud Poile and coach Keith Allen did an excellent job in the expansion draft, selecting players such as goalies Parent and Favell, defensemen Watson and Ed Van Impe, and right winger Gary Dornhoefer.

Parent, Watson, Van Impe, and Dornhoefer would become fixtures when the Flyers won consecutive Stanley Cups in 1974 and 1975.

The Flyers were in the West Division with the five other expansion teams. The East Division was composed of teams from the NHL's Original Six.

Fans were slow to accept the new team. Tickets were $2 to $5.50 per game during that first season, and just 7,812 showed up for the home opener. Gradually, as the Flyers sprinkled in wins against the original teams, attendance picked up. By February, they had their first home sellout.

The Flyers finished 31–32–11 in their first season, were outscored by 179–173, and won the title in the West, which was also composed of expansion teams from St. Louis, Oakland, Pittsburgh, Minnesota, and Los Angeles.

That was the first step, a baby step, toward the 1974 Stanley Cup championship.

The Flyers have won just two Cups in their history, and none since 1975. But they *have* been successful. Entering the 2016–17 season, they had missed the playoffs just 10 times and had reached the Cup Finals eight times.

Since they entered the NHL in 1967–68, only Montreal and Boston have a higher points percentage than the Flyers.

That, and the players' eagerness to live in the community and get involved in local charity events, explains why a sellout crowd attended the alumni game to help celebrate the franchise's 50th anniversary.

Boucher was asked if he was surprised by the huge turnout.

"I don't know why I would be shocked because I know how great of a hockey town this is," he said. "Everybody talks about a sports town; it's a great hockey town. These Flyers fans, starting right around this time of year, working into February, March…they really get jacked up to watch their Flyers play into the spring."

Boucher paused.

"I've had a couple of opportunities to be a part of teams that did that," he said. "I know what it's all about, so I guess that I'm not shocked that 19,000 fans came to watch their heroes of yesterday play because they love the Flyers so much, and it's a real treat as a player when you're all done to get another chance to be back in the NHL for one night. It was a real special night."

"I think it's the only city in the league that would do that, on the hockey scene at least," Clarke, 67, the greatest player in franchise history, said about the alumni game sellout. "I mean, there are still some good players to watch like Lindros, LeClair, and Briere. Those guys are still pretty good players, but there are a lot of us that aren't. It was really fun, though."

Lindros kidded that he fans got to watch old players perform "in slow motion."

"It's great when you get in front of that crowd that's always behind you for five decades now," he added. "All the guys had wonderful stories about the support they've gotten along the way and their own journeys and the team's success. The fans are a really big part of it and you could feel it."

Ed Snider would have been proud.

Roller-Coaster Season

The alumni game was a great time, and it was an honor for me to be a part of it. It was a chance to celebrate the "good ol' days," and forget briefly about the puzzling 2016–17 Flyers, a team that had been on a wild roller coaster ride.

We won 10 straight from November 27 to December 14, equaling the third-longest winning streak in franchise history. Jake Voracek, Claude Giroux, Brayden Schenn, and Wayne Simmonds were our top forwards, rookie Ivan Provorov keyed the defense, and Steve Mason handled most of the goaltending duties during the winning streak, which solidified our grasp of an Eastern Conference playoff spot.

When we won our 10th straight on December 14, only three NHL teams (Chicago, Montreal, and Pittsburgh) had more points than the Flyers. At the time, we had a nine-point cushion over ninth-seeded Tampa Bay in the East.

But right around the alumni game, we went on a skid that saw us lose 12 out of 15, putting the playoffs in jeopardy as the season inched past the midway point.

To be honest, I didn't think we would be contenders for the Stanley Cup in 2016–17. Before the season, I thought there were three levels of NHL teams—the top group, a middle group, and a group of noncontenders. I figured we were somewhere in the middle of the middle group. I didn't think we'd make a serious run at the Cup, but if you make the playoffs and your goalie gets hot, anything can happen.

The problem was our goalies, Mason and Michal Neuvirth, were not playing at a high level in the season's first month, and the offense was very streaky. Add a defense that had some young players who were still learning—and developing—and you could understand why we were having our ups and downs.

The 10-game winning streak was the franchise's longest since 1985, and it gave us a big boost, but then we went out West and that seems to give us problems, year in and year out. This season was no different.

We had an odd bye week a little past the halfway mark of the season. That gave the players a chance to get away and forget about hockey for four or five days. I know our coach, Dave Hakstol, would have preferred playing because he wanted the players to work out of the slump. But the NHL made the break mandatory—no practices for four days—so the players weren't permitted to have any organized team practices.

Some of our leaders pressed during our skid, most notably our captain, Giroux, who went into the break with just one goal in his last 17 games. When you go into a slump like that, I think you try to do more than you're capable of doing. You start pressing and then it snowballs. You carry the puck longer because you want to make a play, or you pass when you have a wide-open shot because you feel snakebitten and want to give a teammate a good scoring chance. The really great players know how to limit the inevitable slumps, and G is such a hard worker that I don't think anyone expected it to last much longer.

Unfortunately, it did.

Earlier in the season, I don't think many people had seen our 10-game winning streak coming. I include myself in that group.

We could do no wrong in those 10 games. When our goaltender had an off night, our offense bailed him out. When our attack sputtered and didn't generate many scoring chances, our goaltending was excellent.

Mason had eight of the 10 wins and had a 2.33 goals-against average and .926 save percentage during the streak. Clearly, he resembled the goalie who sparked us to a playoff berth the previous season. Rookie Anthony Stolarz started the streak with his first victory (vs. Calgary) in his NHL debut and he also contributed his first career shutout, a 1–0 win in Detroit—the final game we ever played at Joe Louis Arena, a place they fondly call the Joe and which was demolished in 2017.

In the win over Calgary, Stolarz became the first New Jersey–born goalie in NHL history. He definitely made the people from Jackson proud.

I did some research, and it turns out I have watched 53 goalies perform for the Flyers since our first season in 1967–68, and it's always a thrill to watch someone make their debut.

Stolie was solid in his debut against Calgary and looked even better in his second game, the 28-save shutout in Detroit. He was rarely out of position and was unflappable whenever there was a rebound.

"He's big. He moves the puck well, and he's been great in practice," said Simmonds after helping set up Schenn's overtime goal to increase the winning streak to nine games. "But practice and games are totally different, and what surprised me the most was how calm he was in all situations back there. He was totally composed."

After Stolie's victory, we won one more game before the streak ended in Dallas 3–1. It was closer than it looks. We trailed 2–1 and put a lot of pressure on the Stars before they secured the win with an empty-net goal.

During the winning streak, we went from four points out of a playoff spot to nine points ahead of our closest pursuer. Voracek had 16 points to lead us during the run, while Giroux had 12 points and was plus-10. Simmonds and Schenn each had six goals during the sport, and Schenn had three game-winners.

Before we went on our first road trip after the Christmas break, general manager Ron Hextall said it was "important not to give back the ground we gained. We have to keep pushing here."

We went 0–2–1 on that trip, losing in St. Louis, San Jose, and Anaheim (in a shootout). Three weeks after Hexy made that statement, our skid had reached 3–9–3 and we had fallen out of our playoff spot.

Quite frankly, I don't think we were as good as some thought during our 10–0 run and, at the same time, we weren't as bad as it appeared while winning just three of our next 15 games. Confidence is a big part of this game, and we didn't have much when we resumed our schedule in late January.

You could see that guys were pressing and trying to do more than they were capable of doing. That was evident in our longest homestand of the season—five games that stretched to February 11. We did a great job of tightening up the defense, but we managed a total of just five goals (excluding an empty-netter) in those five games, leaving little margin of error for our goalies.

We went 2–2–1 in those five home games and, at the time, we were tied with Toronto for the Eastern Conference's last playoff spot, though the Maple Leafs had two games in hand.

We were in a similar position in 2015–16. That season, we went 17–6–4 from February 16 until the end of the year, enabling us to sneak into the playoffs in the next-to-last regular-season game.

But there would be no repeat of our magical run. We finished 2016–17 with a 39–33–10 record and 88 points—eight fewer points than the previous season. We finished seven points behind Toronto, the Eastern Conference's last wild-card team.

The Flyers thus became the first team in NHL history to miss the playoffs during a season in which it had a 10-game winning streak.

We were great at home (25–11–5) and not so great on the road (14–22–5). If we could have played just .500 on the road, we would have been in the playoffs.

Our offense deserted us. We averaged a healthy 3.2 goals in our first 32 games, but that dipped to 2.2 goals over our last 50 games.

In other words, our goalies had to play almost flawlessly, and it's difficult to play under those conditions.

"The well went dry," right winger Wayne Simmonds, who led the team with 31 goals, said about our overall drop in production. "I don't know how to explain it. I felt like we were getting opportunities, good scoring chances in good areas, and we just couldn't put the puck in the net. Eventually that was our downfall.…I think toward the end of the year we started getting it back, we started putting more pucks in the back of the net, and I think that's more indicative of our team."

The Flyers had a 19–10–3 record when they won their 10th straight game on December 14. At that point, they had more points than Washington, which finished with an NHL-leading 118 points.

From that point, however, we won just 20 of our final 50 games (20–23–7) and scored 110 goals. Only New Jersey and Colorado scored fewer in that span.

Our offense did improve late in the season when Jordan Weal was promoted from the AHL's Lehigh Valley Phantoms and Valtteri Filppula was acquired from Tampa Bay. That gave the lines much more balance.

"We started making plays when they were there and started making better decisions," captain Claude Giroux said. "It's like we didn't have a bus on our shoulder when we had the puck. We just played hockey."

Giroux finished with just 14 goals, but wasn't himself for a huge part of the season because he was recovering from hip and abdominal surgeries. I'm looking forward to seeing him play a full season totally healthy. When healthy, G has been one of the league's most productive players.

Looking back on 2016–17, it was a strange season. We had so much promise during our winning streak, but things just went sour after that. It was a disappointing year, but the silver lining is that the future is bright for this team. We saw the maturation of several young players—including Ivan Provorov, Travis Konecny and Weal—and we should have some promising additions from the Phantoms in the lineup next season.

Defensemen Sam Morin and Robert Hagg were recalled from Lehigh Valley and made impressive NHL debuts late in the season.

They could be in the lineup in 2017–18, and we also have gifted defensive prospects Travis Sanheim and Phil Myers working their way toward the big-league team, so our defense should be terrific down the road.

With Ed Snider, Bernie Parent, and many other pivotal Flyers figures.

CHAPTER 12
OUTDOOR HOCKEY

W hile lying on a St. Croix beach in the US Virgin Islands during the 2017 All-Star break, my mind drifted to…the frigid outdoors, for some reason.

Specifically, I started thinking back to playing hockey outside as kids and the great memories we created on frozen ponds.

All of which is a roundabout way of broaching my next subject: outdoor NHL hockey.

It started with Montreal's 4–3 win over host Edmonton before 57,167 frozen fans at Commonwealth Stadium in 2003.

How cold was it?

It was minus-7 degrees, and hot chicken soup was served on the Canadiens' bench.

Montreal goaltender Jose Theodore, wore a *bleu, blanc, et rouge* tuque over his helmet to try to combat the brutal conditions.

The conditions were also nasty when Buffalo hosted the Penguins in the snowy Winter Classic at Ralph Wilson Stadium on New Year's Day in 2008.

A crowd of 71,217 watched the Penguins emerge with a 2–1 shootout victory. Sidney Crosby scored the game-winner in a game that is fondly remembered because of the mounds of snow on the ice. Combined with the snowfall, it contributed to the merry, innocent atmosphere that filled the stadium. The fans were watching professional players feel as if they were little kids playing on a neighborhood pond.

That was the Winter Classic at its freezing best.

The same feeling was evident when it started snowing while we were practicing at historic Fenway Park—the players, led by Scott Hartnell, had a snowball fight on the ice the day before our first outdoor game.

With my sons, Jeff and Matt, and the Geico Caveman at the Winter Classic in Boston in 2010.

The game was played on New Year's Day 2010, and we lost a 2–1 overtime decision to the Boston Bruins in the same ballpark where Carton Fisk waved his homer fair down the left field line to win Game 6 of the 1975 World Series.

Marco Sturm's overtime goal gave the Bruins the comeback victory.

"It's probably going to be my most memorable goal ever, and I'm going to enjoy it," Sturm said.

Sturm was right. He was with four NHL teams over the next two years and scored a total of eight goals in those seasons before his career ended.

But he would always have that game-winning Winter Classic goal against Michael Leighton in 2010.

Danny Syvret, of all people, had given us a 1–0 second-period lead by scoring the first goal of his career.

But former Flyer Mark Recchi tied it on a power-play goal, deflecting Derek Morris' pass past Leighton with 2:18 left in regulation.

We only got a point, but it was an outstanding event, and there must have been at least 8,000 Flyers fans who made the trip to Fenway, adding to the festive atmosphere.

Winter Classic, Part II

We played in our second Winter Classic on January 2, 2012, losing 3–2 to the New York Rangers at Citizens Bank Park. Our third outdoor appearance was a 4–2 loss in Pittsburgh at Heinz Field on February 25, 2017.

Truth be told, I actually enjoyed our 2011 alumni game at Citizens Bank Park more than our three official outdoor games.

It was New Year's Eve, 32 years after his Hall of Fame career ended, and white-haired Bernie Parent was flawless as the Flyers edged the New York Rangers 3–1 in the Winter Classic alumni game at sold-out Citizens Bank Park.

In a four-minute stint in which he stopped all six shots he faced—including one on Ron Duguay's breakaway—the 66-year-old Parent was saluted by the electric crowd of 45,808.

Some had seen him during his heyday. Others had only watched him in videos or read about his dominance.

As he skated off the ice after his crowd-hugging appearance, chants of "Bernie, Bernie, Bernie" echoed around the orange-strewn ballpark. The crescendo built as fans, young and old—many of whom

With Flyers broadcaster Steve Coates at the Winter Classic at Citizens Bank Park in 2012.

weren't even born when Parent led the Flyers to Stanley Cups in 1974 and 1975—joined forces.

If you shut your eyes, it was easy to imagine you were sitting in the venerable Spectrum during the days of leisure suits, 45-cents-a-gallon gas prices, and the disco rage.

Bernie, Bernie, Bernie.

"I was fortunate that they went easy on me," a smiling Parent said of the Rangers.

Bernie was asked what he was thinking as Duguay—who drew whistles when introduced, just like old times—came in on a breakaway.

215

"I said, 'Lord, save me one more time,' and he did," he said.

Said Duguay, "I wasn't going to pick the top corner on him."

Bernie said his training was limited because he had had shoulder-replacement surgery in June, and he added it was nice for some of the older fans to "rekindle" the magic of the mid-1970s.

"It seems like it happened yesterday," he said.

Tweeted one fan: "Who starts in the Classic? Bob, Bryz, or Bernie?"

The fan was referring to Sergei Bobrovsky, Ilya Bryzgalov, and Parent. (Bobrovsky got the start.)

Bernie became emotional when someone mentioned the fans chanting his name.

"I don't know how to describe it," he said. "I guess the best way to describe it is, the feeling you get when people chant your name, money cannot buy. Any amount of money cannot buy that. You know what? You look at this, it's one big family who got together today. It's not the team. It's the people from Philly and it's one big family, and we enjoyed the whole thing as a family."

After the game, Bernie said to me in that beautiful French-Canadian accent of his, "That Dugauy. He's a classy guy."

He hit Bernie right in the pads with his shot.

* * *

It was a wonderful day. I knew most of the alumni players on both teams from being around so long, and I just remember how much fun I had, the fans had, and the players had. They were like little kids again.

For the alumni game, I got to do in-game interviews for the big scoreboard at Citizens Bank Park. And I was the public-address guy for that game—I sat between the benches—and got to announce goals by John LeClair, Shjon Podein, and Mark Howe.

Mark called the game a "celebration of hockey" for the fans. "When I was a player here, Bernie was the goalie coach, so it's an honor," Howe said. "One of the reasons I was so happy to do this is because I've never put on the blades with Bernie."

At practice a day earlier, defenseman Joe Watson, an original Flyer who was 68 at the time and the oldest player on either alumni team, grabbed a can of beer and pronounced, "Boys, here's your protein!"

I guess it worked, because they beat a much younger Rangers team.

Bernie was in his glory after the game.

"I'm still in my prime," he cracked.

It was a beautiful thing.

* * *

One of the cool things about the Winter Classic alumni game was how the much-publicized feud between Bob Clarke and Eric Lindros ended.

Before then, it had been a little sketchy. I remember when we closed the Spectrum, they skated together. It wasn't like they were holding hands going around the ice, but I think that was the first time there seemed to be the possibility that past problems had a chance of being resolved.

About a half hour before the alumni game, Eric was shown on the jumbo screen and the crowd erupted in cheers. The ovation was even louder during the pregame introductions.

"I had a good time and it was real nice to get back in town and hear that," Lindros said after the game. "I didn't know what to expect. It was really special."

Bernie was impressed by the crowd's enthusiastic response to Lindros.

"I thought it was awesome," he said. "Let's remember, the first two or three years he played, he was the best hockey player in the world before he got hurt."

Eric was 38 at the alumni game, and he revealed that, a short time later, then–general manager Paul Holmgren wanted him to return to the Flyers as a player.

Because of numerous concussions suffered during his career with the Flyers, Toronto, Rangers, and Dallas, Eric had retired after the 2006–07 season.

He admitted he was stunned by Holmgren's offer. Despite Lindros' age and medical history, Holmgren thought he could help the Flyers, especially on the power play.

"Are you nuts?" Lindros said he replied when Holmgren made the offer.

Lindros said he was "amazed" when Holmgren asked him if he was interested in making a comeback. He said Holmgren was taking about how they had the cap space to make it work.

"I think he was pretty serious," Lindros said.

Holmgren had been impressed by Lindros' performance in the alumni game at Citizen Bank Park.

"I think he had the worst seat in the house," Lindros cracked. "I don't know what game he was watching."

Lindros was asked if he ever considered the offer to return.

"Oh, God! Oh!!!!!!!"

That was a definitive "no."

* * *

While at practice the day before the alumni game, Eric said he had put his feud with Clarke behind him. Clarke said the same thing after the game.

"We had our battles, but once he was gone it was over, I thought," Clarke said. "We're all Philadelphia Flyers."

Eric and Clarkie had a nice, cordial conversation about numerous topics, including training tips.

Eric was a six-time All-Star with the Flyers and won the Hart Trophy as the NHL MVP in the 1994–95 season.

"Once Eric was gone, the wounds were over as far as we were concerned," Clarke said.

Clarkie said he would "always campaign for him to be in the Hall of Fame."

In 2016, Eric was inducted.

Bryz the Comic

I wasn't a big Ilya Bryzgalov fan, but I will say this: he was always good for some laughs.

The day before we played the New York Rangers in the 2012 Winter Classic in Philadelphia, it seemed more like a comedy routine than an impromptu news conference in the Flyers' locker room at Citizens Bank Park.

That's where Bryzgalov revealed that backup Sergei Bobrovsky would be the team's starting goalie the next day.

"I have great news and even better news," said Bryzgalov, who had lost four straight and struggled through most of the season. "Great news: I'm not playing [in the Winter Classic]. And good news: we have a chance to win the game."

Bryz was mocking himself for his poor play. Signed to a nine-year, $51 million contract before the season, he had a 3.01 goals-against average and .890 save percentage at the time.

In his last four games before the Winter Classic, Bryz had a 4.58 goals-against average and an .816 save percentage.

He obviously wasn't earning his paycheck.

"It's not the end of the universe," Bryzgalov said of being benched.

Bobrovsky had been on a hot streak at the time, going 5–1 with two no-decisions in his previous eight games, along with a 1.55 goals-against average and .947 save percentage in that span.

In the Flyers' locker room, the players said they still had confidence in Bryzgalov, but virtually all of them seemed pleased Bobrovsky was getting the nod.

"Bryz has maybe had a tough couple games, but Bob has been pretty steady the whole year," high-scoring winger Scott Hartnell said. "I think it might be good for Bryz to get a wake-up call and work on some things and get back to the goalie he can be and that we all know."

Hartnell said he had a "lot of faith" in Bryz. "He's a good man and a great goalie, and he'll be there for us."

"It's totally deserved," center Danny Briere said of Bobrovsky getting the start. "For us, it doesn't matter who's playing, but it's good to see Bob being rewarded for his play."

The players loved Bob's dedication.

"No one outworks him," defenseman Braydon Coburn said.

"This guy probably is the last guy to leave from the practice rink every day. I know, because I'm usually the second-to-last," Coburn said. "He's kind of a little bit of an opposite to Bryz. He's easygoing, and Bryz is a personality."

Bryz was like a stand-up comedian that day.

Asked what he would do during the Winter Classic, he dead-panned, "Make sure I don't forget my thermos. Put some nice tea in and enjoy the bench."

Earl Grey with lemon and very sweet, he added.

Bryzgalov said he was told of the decision by goalie coach Jeff Reese.

"Yes, I'm a human," said Bryzgalov when asked if he was disappointed. "I'm not made from steel, but it is what it is, and I had a good practice again like yesterday and two days ago. We just keep moving forward and lots of games in front of us. Lots of hockey. I heard it was still the main goal in Philadelphia to win the Stanley Cup and prepare for this."

Never a dull moment with Bryz, eh?

Bobrovsky, who was then in his second year with us and would win the Vezina Trophy for the Columbus Blue Jackets after the 2012–13 season, said it didn't matter who started "because the most important thing is the result. It's a real game. It's two points on the line, so it'll be special. But the result is the most important thing."

Ah, the game.

It was billed as Broad Street vs. Broadway. There were snow flurries in the second period, a milestone goal scored by one of the Flyers, and dramatics in the final minute.

But we lost another heartbreaker 3–2 to the New York Rangers.

I was the PA guy for that game, too, but I moved upstairs and had 100 people standing behind me from the networks.

Like Syvret, Brayden Schenn waited until Winter Classic to score the first NHL goal of his career. Schenn and Claude Giroux gave us a 2–0 lead, but the Rangers rallied in a rink that stretched from first to third base.

The Rangers got two goals from Mike Rupp and they secured the win when their great goalie, Henrik Lundqvist, stopped Briere on a penalty shot with 19.6 seconds left. Danny tried to go five-hole, but Lundqvist denied him and made a pad save.

Despite the win, Rangers coach John Tortorella was fuming after the game.

"They called a penalty shot which I still don't understand," he said. "I'm not sure if NBC got together with the refs to turn this into an overtime game. I thought the game was reffed horribly.... In that third period, it was disgusting."

A crowd of 46,967 watched the game in single-digit temperatures.

Shivering in Pittsburgh

Fans were also shivering in our 2017 outdoor game at windswept Heinz Field in Pittsburgh, where we outplayed the Penguins in a lot of areas but dropped a closer-than-it-looks 4–2 decision.

"We had good opportunities, but it's getting old," right winger Jake Voracek said after we lost for the seventh time in our last nine games. "You can play good, but as long as you don't find a way to win a game, nobody really cares."

We outshot the Penguins 38–29 and won 59 percent of the faceoffs. But, as was the case for most of the season, we allowed the first goal and were chasing the game.

"It was a tough result," coach Dave Hakstol said, "I thought our team played well and did a lot of good things, but we walk away with the wrong result."

That statement could have aptly described many of our games in January and February. We outplayed teams in a lot of games, but couldn't finish around the net. It also didn't help that our goalies were frequently outplayed, as was the case in the Stadium Series game against the Penguins. Pittsburgh goalie Matt Murray made 36 saves, while Michal Neuvirth made 25.

It marked the eighth straight game we had outshout our opponent, but we had just a 2–6 record in those contests.

Go figure.

Still, it was a fun and entertaining game. Before the opening faceoff, seven *real* penguins from the Pittsburgh Zoo and PPG Aquarium were let loose and scurried about on the auxiliary rink, adjacent the rink where the game was played. The fans, naturally, loved it—especially when one of the penguins fell down but popped right back up.

Gritty little guy. He had a little bit of Ian Laperriere in him.

When the game started, there were lots of back-and-forth chants from the Penguins and Flyers fans. The air was filled with intermittent snow flurries—and there were lots of Terrible Towels waved by the Steelers, er, Penguins fans.

The players loved playing in the outdoors, and there were thousands of orange jerseys in the crowd.

"Everybody has great memories of growing up and playing outdoors. It takes you back to the heart of the game," Hakstol said,

"It felt awesome," winger Wayne Simmonds said, referring to playing outdoors, not the result. "It's the way ice hockey should be played."

Simmonds said he couldn't help notice the crowd.

"I saw a lot of orange in the stands, so we were represented well," he said. "We have the greatest fans in hockey."

The matchup, played in the bitter cold between bitter cross-state rivals, was shown on NBC. It averaged nearly two million viewers and was the most-watched NHL regular-season game in three years, excluding Winter Classics, according to the Nielsen Company.

"It's good for the game," general manager Ron Hextall said. "People watch an outdoor game because there's something about them. They're neat to watch."

All day and night, the restaurants and pubs near the stadium were flooded with people wearing their Flyers or Penguins jerseys. The event had an Army-Navy feel to it. We have such a great rivalry with the Penguins, and it's good for the state and good for the NHL.

"I don't know if I've ever had more fun playing in a game," said Penguins center Matt Cullen, 40, after scoring what turned out to be the winning goal.

* * *

At first, I was a big proponent of outdoor games. What could be better than having a bunch of grown men going back to their little-boy roots and playing an NHL game outside?

But through the years, the outdoor games have lost some of their unique nature. There were six of them in the 2013–14 season, for instance. In the 2016–17 season, there were four. Too many, I say. It takes away from the distinctiveness of playing outside. I liked the original concept of the games, but by having so many outdoor games, it's not as special.

All told, there have been 22 outdoor games, including 21 from January 1, 2008 to February 25, 2017. On the latter date, we played the Penguins at Heinz Field, which hosted the 2011 Winter Classic between the Pens and the Washington Capitals.

Fans love the outdoor games. Those 22 outdoor contests averaged an impressive 54,924 fans per game.

We are also slated to meet the Penguins in an outdoor game in 2019 in Philly. It'll be a great time for the fans who attend or watch on TV because, let's face it, the Flyers and Penguins are about as friendly as Donald Trump and Hillary Clinton were on the 2016 campaign trail.

All of which should create great theater.

Family Life

One of the nice parts about my job is that my family has been with me for the entire ride. I've had the chance to expose my wife, Ellen, and our two boys, Matt and Jeff, to hockey, and, like me, they fell in love with the sport. They've been to so many big games over the years and I'd love to have them all in a Stanley Cup parade some year.

Ellen and I got married in 1982, and she didn't know anything at all about hockey until she met me. She used to come to all the games before we had kids, and she became very knowledgeable. She still comes to some games and still enjoys it.

My family is the main reason for whatever success I've had, and it was so great that they were by my side the night I got inducted into the Philadelphia Sports Hall of Fame in 2015.

To this day, I still cannot believe they honored me in such a way, and I am truly humbled to be in the Hall with such icons of the Philadelphia sports world. To think I'm in the Hall amazes me.

The night I went into the Hall of Fame, I had lots of friends who came out. The guys from my neighborhood—I played a lot of football and baseball with them when we were younger—were there. The Southwest Philly boys. They were a lot of fun. They were hooting and hollering and carrying on and I really appreciated them being there. It was such a great night.

With my sons, Jeff and Matt, on the ice at the Spectrum for the Flyers Christmas Skate in 1992.

There are some tremendous athletes who are in the Philadelphia Hall of Fame, including Bobby Clarke, Bernie Parent, Wilt Chamberlain, Mike Schmidt, Joe Frazier, and Chuck Bednarik.

I was inducted on the same night as Dick Vermeil, Rick MacLeish, Garry Maddox, Timmy Brown, Rich Gannon, and Walt Hazzard, among others.

The thing that made it even extra special for me was that Dave Zinkoff, the legendary 76ers public address announcer from back in the day, went into the Hall posthumously that night. I knew Zink and would talk with him when we occasionally played our games back-to-back. He was an interesting guy. He was the Show. The team was terrible for a while, but he was the man who kept everybody entertained.

I remember being in a wedding in Ocean City many years ago. One of the off-ice NHL officials invited us, and we sat with the Zink, who was friends with him, too. At that time, it was preseason for both the NHL and the NBA. If I remember correctly, the Sixers had won their first two exhibition games and we had won our first three. So at one point in the wedding, Zink goes up and talks to the band. And the bandleader hands Zink the mic, and he says in that distinctive and well-known voice of his: "Ladies and gentlemen, I'm sitting here with Lou Nolan, and we are the two undefeated announcers in Philadelphia." It was the *preseason*! But that was Zink. He knew how to make people laugh. The guy was such a witty person. I loved the guy and loved being around him.

Getting back to the Hall of Fame night. I had to make a speech, and it made me think back to some of the crazy things that have happened during my career with the Flyers. I did miss a few games during these 50 years, whether it was for laryngitis or for a rare conflict with my job selling securities for Austin Atlantic Capital.

While working on my speech, I also recalled the time my announcing career briefly passed before my eyes. That was the night a puck hit me and I became disoriented and didn't know where I was.

I used to have a microphone and be able to talk to the TV guys during games. I was like the original Pierre McGuire. They would call down to me and I would give a live report from down near the penalty box. They would ask me what the refs were talking about and things like that. But the league eventually put an end to it. They didn't want me to give the reports. I guess I told them the refs screwed up or something.

But before the league ended my live reports, I was working down there one night at the Spectrum in the late 1970s and—*bing!*—I get hit right in the head with a deflected pass or shot. This was before we had glass in front of us, so we were very vulnerable to flying pucks.

I was stunned. Our broadcasters, Gene Hart and Bobby Taylor, were talking to me through my headset. Our producer said, "Louie's hit! Louie's hit!" I was dazed, and the next thing I heard was Bobby Taylor's voice: "Let's go downstairs to see if Lou Nolan is feeling okay."

I couldn't talk. My tongue wouldn't work. I tried to talk to them and the words wouldn't come out. Finally, after a few seconds, I blurted out, "Honey, I'm okay." I was talking to my wife, Ellen, who I gathered was watching the game at home. Gradually, I got my bearings and I was okay for the rest of the night, but I was groggy for a while.

Anyway, I got home later that night and figured Ellen was going to meet me at the door with, "How are you, honey? That must have been a scary thing!" But I went inside, and the house was pretty quiet. I walked into our family room, and the TV was on and she was sound asleep on the sofa. It turns out she fell asleep during the game and never even knew I got hit. The nerve!

But, hey, I can't hold it against her. Ellen has always been my biggest supporter. She used to go the games and sit in Section Z, the last row, with Joanie Kadlec, the wife our public relations director, Joe Kadlec, and Gail Colletti (wife of Ned Colletti, who covered the Flyers for the *Journal*) and Joe Watson's first wife, Marianne. The four of them hung out together.

Prior to that, when we first starting dating, I took her to a game, walked her to her seat, and told her I'd meet her there after the game. She really had no idea what I did. After the warm-ups ended, she saw me walk down the chute and then walk across the ice and the fans were chanting "Loooouuuu." Later that night she told me she was thinking, *Where the hell is he going?* We laughed about that later, and she became a big fan and saw a lot of games. When our boys came along in the '80s, she didn't make many games, but she knows her stuff. She can talk hockey with anybody.

Without Ellen's support, I could not have done it. She's the best. And my boys grew up around hockey and they're fans to this day. We're a hockey family. We're all hooked on the sport and it's a big part of our lives.

As I said earlier in this book, I was very fortunate to have met Joe Kadlec 50 years ago. He's the person who steered me on a path to a long and wonderful career with the Flyers. Without Joe, Lou Scheinfeld, and the late, great Ed Snider, my life would have been a lot different.

Instead, I bleed Orange and Black.

APPENDIX

THE FLYERS
THROUGH THE YEARS

Here are 30 memorable dates
in the Flyers' history:

June 6, 1967: The Flyers selected 20 players in the NHL expansion draft.

June 12, 1969: The franchise would forever be changed when the Flyers chose Bobby Clarke from the Flin Flon Bombers in the second round (17th overall) of the 1969 draft.

May 15, 1973: The Flyers brought back goalie Bernie Parent, acquiring him and a second-round draft pick from Toronto for Doug Favell and a first-round draft choice.

May 9, 1974: Clarke scored in overtime—some call it the biggest goal in Flyers history—to beat Boston 3–2 and even the Stanley Cup Finals at one game apiece. It was the Flyers' first win in Boston since 1967, ending an 18-game drought (0–16–2) and making them believe they could bring home the Cup.

May 19, 1974: The Flyers, in just their seventh season, became the first expansion team to win the Stanley Cup. With Kate Smith appearing in person to perform "God Bless America," they nipped visiting Boston as Rick MacLeish scored the winner in a Cup-clinching, 1–0 Game 6 victory. Parent had the shutout and won the Conn Smythe Trophy as the playoffs MVP.

May 27, 1975: The Flyers won their second straight Cup as Parent became the first player in NHL history to win the Conn Smythe Trophy in consecutive seasons. Parent had the shutout in the

Cup-clinching 2–0 victory in Buffalo, and Bob Kelly scored the winning goal.

January 11, 1976: The Flyers became the first NHL team to defeat the touring Soviet Army team from the USSR 4–1 at the Spectrum. Joe Watson scored a shorthanded goal in a game in which the Soviets briefly left the ice because of a hit by Ed Van Impe.

May 16, 1976: Montreal defeated the Flyers 5–3 at the Spectrum to sweep the Stanley Cup Finals. Conn Smythe winner Reggie Leach scored 19 goals in 16 playoff games to give him 80 goals (61 on the season), becoming the first player to ever reach that plateau.

December 11, 1977: Tom Bladon set an NHL record for points by a defenseman (eight) as he collected four goals and four assists in an 11–1 win over the Cleveland Barons (remember them?) at the Spectrum.

January 6, 1980: The Flyers defeated host Buffalo 4–2 to increase their unbeaten string to 35 games, the longest streak in professional sports history. (The streak ended January 7 with a 7–1 loss in Minnesota.)

May 24, 1980: The Flyers lost to the host New York Islanders in overtime 5–4 in the decisive Game 6 of the Stanley Cup Finals. A blown referee's call, which led to an Islanders goal, added mystique (and frustration) to the loss.

September 25, 1984: Parent became the first Flyer inducted into the Hockey Hall of Fame.

November 11, 1985: Goalie Pelle Lindbergh, one of the NHL's rising stars, died in a car accident in Somerdale, New Jersey. He was 26.

March 17, 1987: Tim Kerr set a Flyers record with his fourth consecutive 50-goal season.

May 28, 1987: J.J. Daigneault scored with 5:32 left to give the Flyers a 3–2 win over Edmonton and force Game 7 of the Stanley Cup Finals. The crowd's roar generated by the goal was among the loudest ever at the Spectrum. Three days later, the Oilers won Game 7 3–1 in Edmonton. Ron Hextall was named the Conn Smyth winner.

December 8, 1987: Hextall became the first NHL goalie to score a goal by shooting the puck into the opposing net as the Flyers beat Boston 5–2 at the Spectrum.

June 30, 1992: The Flyers were awarded the rights to 19-year-old Eric Lindros by an arbitrator, completing a blockbuster deal with Quebec. The Rangers had also made a trade for Lindros.

May 12, 1996: Florida scored a 2–1 overtime win over the Flyers in an Eastern Conference playoff game. It was the Flyers' final game at the venerable Spectrum.

October 5, 1996: The Flyers fell to Florida 3–1 in the first game ever played at what was then known as the CoreStates Center.

May 4, 2000: Keith Primeau scored in the fifth overtime, giving the Flyers a 2–1 win in Pittsburgh, tying the Eastern Conference semifinals at two games apiece. It was the longest game in NHL history (152:01).

September 20, 2001: Nine days after 9/11, the Flyers and visiting Rangers played to a 2–2 tie in an exhibition game suspended after two periods so everyone in attendance could watch President George W. Bush's emotional address to Congress, which was televised in the arena.

April 11, 2010: Claude Giroux scored the decisive shootout goal and Brian Boucher outdueled Henrik Lundqvist as the Flyers edged the visiting New York Rangers 2–1 to clinch a playoff berth on the last day of the regular season. Matt Carle scored late in regulation to force overtime.

May 14, 2010: The Flyers became the third team in NHL history to overcome a 3–0 series deficit as they defeated host Boston 4–3 in Game 7. Simon Gagne scored the game-winner with 7:08 left as the Flyers overcome a 3–0 deficit in the final game.

June 9, 2010: Patrick Kane scored the game-winner in overtime as Chicago defeated the host Flyers 4–3 and clinched the Stanley Cup in six games. It marked the sixth straight time the Flyers had lost in the Finals.

June 23, 2011: The Flyers traded the faces of the franchise—centers Mike Richards and Jeff Carter—to Los Angeles and Columbus, respectively. They also signed free-agent Ilya Bryzgalov. The trades brought Wayne Simmonds, Jake Voracek, and Brayden Schenn to the Flyers, along with draft picks that turned out to be Sean Couturier and Nick Cousins.

February 4, 2014: Keith Allen, the first coach in franchise history and, as general manager, the architect of the teams' two Stanley Cups, died at age 90.

May 7, 2014: Paul Holmgren was promoted to club president and Ron Hextall was named the team's general manager.

February 20, 2016: Defenseman Shayne Gostisbehere scored the overtime winner against Toronto and set an NHL record for a rookie defenseman by collecting a point in 15 straight games.

April 11, 2016: Flyers co-founder and chairman Ed Snider died after a two-year battle with bladder cancer. He was 83.